Get People to Do What You Want

Get People to Do What You Want

How to Use Body Language and Words to Attract People You Like and Avoid the Ones You Don't

By Gregory Hartley and
Maryann Karinch

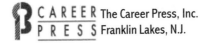
CAREER The Career Press, Inc.
PRESS Franklin Lakes, N.J.

GET PEOPLE TO DO WHAT YOU WANT
EDITED AND TYPESET BY GINA TALUCCI
Cover design by Ian Shimkoviak/Alian Design
Printed in the U.S.A. by Book-mart Press

To order this title, please call toll-free 1-800-CAREER-1 (NJ and Canada: 201-848-0310) to order using VISA or MasterCard, or for further information on books from Career Press.

The Career Press, Inc., 3 Tice Road, PO Box 687,
Franklin Lakes, NJ 07417
www.careerpress.com

Library of Congress Cataloging-in-Publication Data
Hartley, Gregory.
    Get people to do what you want : how use body language and words to attract people you like and avoid ones you don't /by Gregory Hartley and Maryann Karinch.
        p. cm.
    Includes index.
    ISBN 978-1-56414-993-0
        1. Body language. 2. Persuasion (Psychology) 3. Influence (Psychology) I. Karinch, Maryann. II. Title.

BF637.N66H375 2008
153.8'52--dc22

2008009474

Dedication

Both of us dedicate this book to Michael Dobson.

Acknowledgments

How in the world could I ever do what I do without the consistent, loving, and intelligent support I get from Jim McCormick? Thank you! And to you, Greg, my wonderful writing partner, I appreciate you as an inventive thinker, an inspiration to me from the first sentence to the last, and a great friend. Thanks also to my patient and helpful "sister," Mary Hemphill, who finds the most amazing ways to make my life easier when I'm stressed out. My mom and my brother, Karl, also show their support in creative and practical ways and never seem to tire of it—I'm blessed to have you as family. Once again, Greg and I have the great privilege of thanking the Career Press team, specifically, Ron Fry, Michael Pye, Kristen Parkes, Kirsten Dalley, Gina Talucci, and Laurie Kelly-Pye. Finally, thanks to my dear friends who help keep me balanced and productive.

— Maryann

Thanks to the enthusiastic team at Career Press who believed this was a good idea even before I did. Career Press has made life easy for both of us, and the entire staff is a pleasure to work with.

I could not have found time to write this book without the help of Max Wood—thanks. Stumbling into Don Landrum at the start of my interrogation career led me to some of the conclusions in this book, whether he knew it or not. Thanks to Dina for keeping me centered and to Mike for helping keep things going when I cannot be around. Thanks to Maryann for following my rambling as I put these very difficult concepts that feel instinctive to me into words others can understand.

Every concept we discuss here is playing out in interrogation rooms around the world as professional interrogators apply these concepts to get others to tell them the truth. The few rank amateurs who have resorted to the unspeakable have tarnished the reputation of these professionals who protect you on a daily basis. These professional interrogators oftenfind the danger and report it before it is too late, but cannot ever disclose it ever happened. To these people who protect the good citizens of the world from the unthinkable, I am grateful.

—Greg

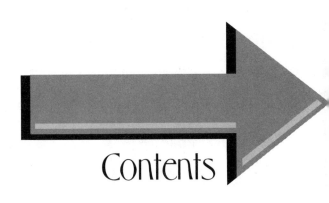

Contents

Section III: Applying the Tools

Introduction

Any book that teaches how to get people to do what you want is a book about manipulation. To manipulate people, you need to understand first what drives them.

A quick look across the spectrum of humanity reveals that humans are complex creatures. Even in the psychologically healthy bands of the spectrum, human beings run the gamut from altruists to curmudgeons. Within this very complex and diverse population, however, there are also recurrent themes; these form the foundation for this book. It is a Machiavellian look at how to make people do what you want, so by its nature, it is dark. If Vincent Price had written *How to Win Friends and Influence People*, this would be that book.

Similar to our primate cousins, humans have a burning desire for companionship. First and foremost, we are herd animals with an instinct to belong that cannot be overlooked. Once we gain that acceptance, however, we push more and more to set ourselves apart. Merely being a member of the crowd is generally not good enough. We want to hold distinction within the group—to be a member with clout at the least, or perhaps even the alpha in the pack. After striving to raise our level of importance within this group, when we achieve that and become a "big fish in a small pond," most of us look for more. We aim to expand our circle to move into a new pond, one with a new group to which we can belong, only to start the process all over again.

If you doubt this premise, think about why you picked up the book. Are you moving into a new group and trying to better adapt and gain acceptance? Or are you looking to differentiate yourself from the crowd? Whether it is at work or in a social group, these two forces drive your choices at this moment, and other people around you are making daily decisions the same way. This book is about understanding those forces, and making conscious decisions that will get the outcomes you want.

One added benefit of learning these tools is the ability to see how and when people such as politicians and advertisers are manipulating you. Even if you never exercise the skills of influence we cover in this book, you will benefit greatly by other people's deliberate attempts to use them.

—Greg Hartley

SECTION I

The Dynamics of
Human Interaction

CHAPTER 1

Shared Needs: Belonging and Differentiating

Take a minute and ponder what elements of your life you cannot live without. Look at the things that make your life valuable; not your latest gadget or miracle cosmetic, but the essentials that would leave a marked void if they disappeared. Some go without saying, such as your most basic human needs: food, clothing, and shelter. But what are the others? In terms of human drives, what is your most basic need—the intangible equivalent of food, clothing, and shelter?

Regardless of whether your personality bends toward introverted or extroverted, regardless of whether your feelings about people make you a misanthrope or philanthropist, human companionship is a primary driver of human behavior. Companionship can be different things to different people, but the premise remains consistent for all but the most deviant minds: people need people.

The Hierarchy of Needs

In 1943, psychologist Abraham Maslow introduced his theory on the Hierarchy of Needs. The ground floor of his pyramid of needs is composed of the biological ones we all know: food, sleep, sex, and other elements essential to life. One floor up, you find all of the things that provide safety. Arguably each of these first two can be met without the need for other people, but the ability to go it alone ends there. Just above that, you have that spectrum of intangibles that relate to belonging and love: affection, relationships, camaraderie. Moving up to the fourth level, you find esteem needs, such as achievement and reputation; and at the top, self-actualization.

Maslow described these needs as a hierarchy because a human being cannot progress to the next tier until the needs below it are met. Therefore, achievement and reputation can come only when someone feels as though he belongs. The personal growth and fulfillment associated with self-actualization can only come after satisfying the need for achievement and reputation.

Stop here for just one minute, because grasping the hierarchy of human needs is the core of the how-to information in this book. The motivation behind a person's choices takes shape according to what lower needs have been met and what higher needs remain to be met. Among the most interesting attributes of human behavior is that these needs are often more

$\bigwedge$

Self-Actualization
Personal growth and fulfillment

Esteem Needs
*Achievement, status, responsibility,
and reputation*

Belongingness and Love Needs
*Family, affection, relationships,
work groups, and so on*

Safety Needs
*Protection, security, order, law, limits, stability,
and so on*

Biological and Physiological Needs
*Basic life needs, such as air, food, drink, shelter, warmth,
sex, and sleep*

visible from the outside than the inside. That is, others can clearly see things about you that you cannot, but there are exceptions.

Look at the top tier of self-actualization. How can you see, understand, or manipulate another person's sense of self-actualization? In all of the years I have dealt with peoples' behavior, I have yet to understand how anyone can begin to understand what self-actualization means in another, especially when so few can define it for themselves.

Interrogators rarely try. We are on a schedule. The science of interrogation is about asking questions and getting as much information in as little time as possible. We need shortcuts to get down to business, so we will take the interrogator's approach to confronting a person's progress on the route to self-actualization:

1. Assume the person is not self-actualized. Most people are not.

2. Even if he is, shifting him to one of the lower tiers in the hierarchy will change that quickly. When an interrogator mounts a successful attack on someone's reputation, the ensuing campaign to restore that reputation drops the victim to the level below actualization. If you want to see an everyday example, tune in to the smear campaigns of a presidential election. Watch the effect of defending a reputation that took decades to build. Do you see a different aspect of the otherwise poised candidate?

3. If I want to move him even lower on the pyramid, I attack his sense of belonging. His response as he tries to hold on to this most basic, intangible human need is to drop a step down on the hierarchy. If he is masterful, or well insulated, this re-grounding can be quick, but it allows the manipulator an instant to get the upper hand.

The Drivers:
Belonging and Differentiating

The concept of belonging is simple. Everyone needs to feel as though he has a place in a group, and this does not mean something as superficial as a plot of land in the suburbs with two kids and an SUV. Fundamentally, it means experiencing some kind of bond with others. This can range from a simple configuration of an impromptu group formed to solve a problem to complex fraternal organizations and societies.

As you read this, you may be thinking, "I have bonds, but I'm certainly not the same as my friends, acquaintances, coworkers, and family members. I'm different. Everyone knows that. A lot of them even look up to me for it."

You got to that point by belonging. If you were not accepted first, you would simply be a stranger whose differences would have no meaning and carry no interest for the group. You would not be a subject of discussion in the same way a member of the group would be. Those differences—the identifying traits that you so value—are what I call *differentiating factors*, and they are at the heart of both self-esteem and esteem from others. It is about accomplishments, reputation, status, and responsibility. Regardless of the group, and regardless of what creates the identity of the group, first belonging, and then differentiating, drives the sense of esteem a person gets. The kind of differentiating can be as individual as a fingerprint, and it is heavily dependent on the person's self-image, something that is highly subjective and volatile.

Self-Image

Frame of reference determines our outlook on the world. The more facts we know and the more expansive our experiences, the broader our frame of reference and the more completely we see the picture. That frame of reference puts *you* in the picture somewhere, too.

What do you look like in that picture? You may not have considered how your self-image is tied to others. What other people tell you *about you* colors how you see yourself in the frame. In some cases, they expressed an opinion openly, but in others, they merely implied it—or you thought they did. (Your psyche will sometimes manufacture other people's judgments or opinions of you.)

Start with the physical. Are you taller or shorter than average? For what population? A friend of mine is 5'3", and tells of a time when she was tall. The story is funny, because as a child, she was always tall for her age. Only much later in life, when she told friends she was glad she had been gifted with height, did people burst her bubble. She carried the delusion of being tall well into adulthood. How does such a skewed perspective develop? Her self-image developed as she looked at the tops of her childhood friends' heads, and then it hardened, because those friends had never challenged her as they grew and she didn't. Her height was never a subject of discussion. This same kind of deference occurs on a regular basis when someone differentiates himself in a confined environment and creates a superlative image in a limited population. You see this phenomenon all the time in small-town high schools, where the most gifted football player is some runt who runs fast. As soon as he gets to a college populated by big boys who outsprint him, his self-image takes a beating.

Maybe you are more attractive or athletic than others in your group. Ask yourself what the standard is for your group, and what would happen if your tribe suddenly changed? What if you changed jobs and ended up in the Yucatan Peninsula with Mayan descendants who top out at about 5 feet tall? Or if you took your slightly plump, tanned body—considered beautiful where you live now—for an extended stay in Norway? While this may be a bit of a stretch, it spotlights that your sense of belonging to a group and being distinguished within that group is a relative judgment.

It applies in terms of achievement, too. Many people become big fish in little ponds, and become convinced that they are capable of so much more. They move on to a larger pond only to find that their deferential group has been left behind. Suddenly they are no longer better, or even normal, much less superlative. This new set of expectations, whether vocational or social, changes the ground rules.

Self-Image and Interrogation—the Extremes

The *science* of interrogation is about asking questions and getting as much information in as little time as possible; this assumes the person cooperates. The *art* of interrogation is applying a set of extreme interpersonal skills so subtly that the unskilled observer rarely knows what is going on. Both the interrogator and the source are keenly aware of the interchange; it is more stressful for both than either will likely encounter in any other situation. This art of interrogation relies heavily on managing the person's self-image.

In the interrogation business, our euphemism for a cooperative source is a broken source. This implies that we have broken her will to resist and gotten her to cooperate. We often say a source "broke on direct," which means we asked a question and she answered. No fanfare or manipulation. The mechanics of what makes a person divulge sensitive information to her enemy in that manner cannot be glibly overlooked. Consider this classic scenario of a captured soldier sent to a compound to face an interrogation.

When the soldier enters military service he is indoctrinated, pumped full of duty, honor, country, and camaraderie. This system of teamwork, mission, and higher purpose insulates him from the thought of what the enemy must be like. It is simple: the guy on the other side is the enemy, he is to be destroyed, and we have the power to do it. The soldier's self-image is manufactured and injected into him; regardless of where he fits in the group, he is a soldier. He belongs, so now all he needs to do is differentiate. The younger a soldier, the easier it is to have him absorb this self-image. Camaraderie, cohesive training, good leadership, and proper discipline insulate him and prevent him from needing self-examination. He does not need to evaluate whether he is a fool or a wise man. It doesn't matter whether or not he understands his government's policy and it fits his ideology, or that he is serving more than one master. The profile is built and reinforced by what it takes to stay alive, stay mission-focused, and to look out for his team.

When he is captured, everything turns upside down. He no longer has the input to maintain the image of warrior, professional, and noble servant to his country. As he sees the enemy for the first time in human terms, he is barraged on every front with reality-altering images. The self-image inputs that created his role of soldier recede into oblivion. No longer a combatant, he now depends on the captor for everything from food and shelter to communication with family. The other soldiers from his world are now just as dependent; and the uniforms that held so much power before are gone, or worse yet, simply they are a mocking reminder of the earlier self-image. His only contact with someone who speaks his language is the interrogator, so prisoners often react to questions in an attempt to sustain conversation and regain some form of stability. A good interrogator starts the conversation in such a way that the first question lets the interrogator know whether the system has done the hard work of "breaking" the prisoner for him. In wars prior to the 21st century, most people—as high as 90 percent—have broken on direct, or simply answered the interrogators questions without manipulation. As I often say to people curious about the leverage that interrogators have, we are anxiety brokers relying on the fear of the unknown, and managing that fear to get a desired result. The one unknown that people fear the most is personal extinction—and I do not mean physical death. The personal extinction to which I'm referring is psychological, an aspect of identity similar to self-actualization in that it is so very personal, only the individual knows what defines it. An interrogator's magic is to find the combination of words that engender that fear, and then relieve the fear just as efficiently.

Contrast the scenario of the traditional soldier as a prisoner of war with the current situation involving terrorists. The new enemies of the United States and most of the Western world do not seem to break as readily as the soldier in the traditional mold. And while the enemy has changed, the tools to break him have not. The currently "approved techniques" were derived from a brilliant noncoercive interrogator from Nazi Germany. His techniques, which I discuss later, are brilliant, but they do not seem to have the desired effect on nontraditional combatants. The unsatisfying results are predictable.

The terrorist has no image built on a group of comrades. Often, he operates independently and insulates himself. His self-esteem comes from the fact that he operates clandestinely, and his self-image is deeply rooted in his justification for his actions. When captured, he faces the enemy as a warrior in the cause of a greater power. He sees, often for the first time in his life, the infidel and the experience of capture. That assault on his psyche reinforces the self-image honed by his beliefs, as well as the image of the Western heathen. The true believer gets further justification; he communicates with his centering authority—or in Western terms, he meditates—and the jihadist has his self-image bolstered. There is a cliché that says armies fight their last war continuously. By holding a group of people who face interrogation with these same tools indefinitely, and allowing them to recenter, Western powers have created the unimaginable: the ascetic jihadist. I am not discounting the need for distancing terrorists from their targets, rather I am saying that the Western world needs a different approach for a new enemy. The effect of the current system is to strengthen the self-image of the jihadists and take away any chance the interrogator has to broker anxiety by demonstrating his understanding of the terrorists' feelings of personal extinction.

You will likely never deal with either of these two extremes, but consider what commonalities exist between the interrogator's circumstance and yours. When someone is opposed to you and is bolstered by forces, inside or out, you have little chance to get him to do what you want. But when that person feels threatened—whether the threat is rooted by him feeling like an outsider, feeling like a nobody in the group, or in danger of being supplanted as the alpha—you have a lever. How you apply this lever is the art, because you will creatively rely on both positive and negative levers, depending on the situation and the individual.

I want to emphasize here that it is extremely dangerous to inject poison into someone's self-image. You can push a person to retaliate violently by doing that. If you manipulate someone to the point where she feels she has lost a sense of self—that is, the point of personal extinction—and you do not know how to manage the situation, you can seriously harm her psyche. When interrogators do this, we either pull the person out of it and restore her sense of self, or walk away, not caring what kind of damage we just inflicted. But daily life is not an interrogation, and the outcome is not a life-or-death matter. Used for the right purpose and in proper measure, you can get people to do things you want; used incorrectly, you will see that the use of these tools can result in things you really do not want.

Megan Meier's suicide spotlights a worst-case situation resulting from toying with someone's self-image. As an over-weight, 13-year-old girl she endured taunting from the cool soccer girls about being fat, but also got the occasional invitation to join them for lunch at school. When a boy named Josh Evans—a fictional character created by people who knew her vulnerabilities—expressed strong interest in Megan through MySpace exchanges, she was thrilled. When that same "boy" dumped her with vitriolic rants, she snapped. Megan hung herself—the literal expression that she had experienced personal extinction.

For people ages 15 to 24, suicide is the third leading cause of death, according to the U.S. Centers for Disease Control and Prevention. Their young psyches are not necessarily resilient enough to deal with the end of a love affair or something such as embarrassment. Think embarrassment isn't a strong enough reason to take your own life? After a DUI or relatively minor scrape with the law—that is, something that would not be considered a violation that would ruin a person's life—some people choose suicide instead of the embarrassment of jail. If their pride in being respectable, dignified individuals was fundamental to their personal identity, what the jail time did was drive them to personal extinction. Their definitions of *respectable* and *dignified* did not allow a check mark in the box for incarceration. A quick Google search yields discussions of dozens of recent examples, and many of the people were well into adulthood when they did it.

Self-Image and Cloistered Groups (or Unpredicted Outcomes From Predictable Situations)

Every group develops a norm, or concept of typical, for its group. This norm can be mainstream for the overall culture, or so narrowly focused and bizarre that only initiates recognize it. The more open the group to outsiders, the more mainstream the group will remain. As a group becomes more cloistered, individuals within it gain more power and influence. Cult leaders illustrate this dramatically: Jim Jones of the People's Temple, Charles Manson of the Manson Family, Marshall Applewhite of Heaven's Gate, and David Koresh of the Branch Davidians. Often these "big fish" individuals will distort and convolute the norm of the group so much that by the end—which in these cases, was the end of life—none of the others could recognize how it happened. The people who fell under their spell described them as charismatic, or even divine. One quick look by the rest of us who did not belong to that tribe ask one main question: what the hell were they thinking? Oddly enough, they were responding in the same way Maslow predicted: first by belonging, and then by differentiating.

They belonged because each of them took part in a group. Whether it offered refuge from parents who opposed the

hippie way of life, a world that did not understand racial har-
mony, or simply feeling as though they had no peers in the
real world, each of these people found a group with ideas and
beliefs he or she shared—a place that offered comfort.

They differentiated by following a leader who steadily in-
creased his sway over his "family," and skewed the way the
group's norms took shape. In attempting to fit in, each person
moved further and further from the norms of the society at
large as he or she became similar to the others, and even sought
to become a favorite child to this parental figure. It's unlikely
any of these people signed up to commit mass suicide or multiple homicides, but many of them found themselves doing
exactly that. One could argue that, by virtue of ending their
lives and others' lives so dramatically, they were all mentally
ill, but other events—some controlled experiments and others rooted in common practices—indicate otherwise.

In 1971, psychologist Philip Zimbardo invited a population of healthy, middle-class male college students to participate in a two-week study of the effects of prison life on the
psyche. Arbitrarily, he divided the group of 18 in half: nine
guards and nine prisoners. Zimbardo's team transformed part
of a building on the Stanford University campus into a prison
environment, with the added touch of planting video and audio recording devices so they would monitor what happened.
Upon capture the "prisoners" got treated just as real prisoners would, from hearing their Miranda rights to delousing.
The "guards" received no special training, but knew their job

was to enforce order in the prison and do what they thought was necessary to gain the respect of the inmates. While prisoners wore baggy outfits that looked like dresses, the guards wore khaki uniforms and sunglasses, and they were armed with whistles and billy clubs. Guards worked in three-hour shifts, but prisoners were prisoners around the clock.

Day one passed without incident. By day two, a rebellion broke out. All nine guards came on duty together and decided to quell it with force, which began by spraying the prisoners with a fire extinguisher to subdue them. The effect was an ice burn, causing pain and chapping, and it was enough to give the guards the upper hand. They stripped the prisoners, removed their beds, and threw the ringleaders into solitary confinement.

Day three brought some new tactics by the guards. They split the prisoners emotionally and psychologically by singling out three for good behavior and giving them privileges—such as food and beds—while denying others any comforts. Then to make it clear how much control they really had, they switched the good and bad prisoners. The effect it had was to confuse the prisoners, who then thought some of them had "turned." Distrust grew among them. So while the prisoners became more fractured as a group, the guards bonded. One prisoner cracked so badly in this short period of time that he was released from the experiment. Three days later, after disgusting prisoner abuse such as making them clean toilets with their bare hands, the experiment ended. Thinking that no one monitored the video after normal hours, guards on the night shift had concocted such degrading and pornographic punishments that the researchers knew that normalcy no longer mitigated their behavior.

Zimbardo himself asks on his Website devoted to the prison experiment (*www.prisonexp.org*): "How could intelligent, mentally healthy, 'ordinary' men become perpetrators of evil so quickly?" He concluded the following about the fundamental issues of bonding and fracturing:

> By the end of the study, the prisoners were disintegrated, both as a group and as individuals. There was no longer any group unity; just a bunch of isolated individuals hanging on, much like prisoners of war or hospitalized mental patients. The guards had won total control of the prison, and they commanded the blind obedience of each prisoner.

In hazing rituals, fraternities effect an analogous result by leveraging students' desire to belong, reinforcing the demands of leaders through peer pressure, and shrouding the real nature of the hazing-to-come with secrecy. Many of the abuses that have ended tragically involved pledges being forced to out-drink one another—alcohol, that is. One that occurred at Chico State in 2005, though, involved making pledges drink so much water that one of them, Matthew Carrington, died from water intoxication. You might think, "Well, that's stupid. Why didn't they just say, 'Enough's enough?'" The responsible fraternity brothers did something insidious, most likely without even realizing how effective it would be. They physically isolated two of the pledges and broke then down mentally by stressing them out physically.

What caused each of these "experiments" to go haywire? And what does this have to do with your getting people to do what you want? First let's look at the cause of the failure.

Defining a Group—on the Outside Looking In

The bell curve gives us a simple model for analyzing a group. Within any group you can chose to represent people on a bell curve. The narrative description goes something similar to this:

1. Some are barely members of the group, more tolerated than belonging. They exist on the fringes of the group. Lets call these sub-typical. While others may tolerate them, they are not emulated and most others think, "There but for the grace of God go I." They may be discussed, however, because even though they are ugly babies, they are "our ugly babies."

2. Other members represent what is normal, or typical, for the group. No extraordinary abilities. Not particularly charismatic. Just middle of the road, or in our bell-curve image, middle of the line.

3. On the side opposite the ugly babies are people who are super-typical within the group. They are the "beautiful people," admired and emulated, and even obeyed in some cases. Depending on the size of the group, this might be one person or many.

These are the leaders, whether that's a formal or informal designation.

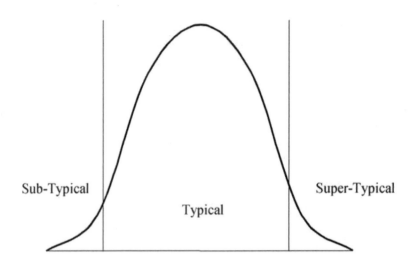

Cloistering to Limit Inputs to Self-Image

Think about this bell-curve model as it applies to your life, on a small scale describing your family all the way up though a full-blown cultural model. We emulate the people on the right. The mainstream model in the American culture results in celebrity endorsement of products. But why does this work?

Humans are primates. That does not necessarily mean you came from monkeys, just that you are a different kind of monkey. It makes no difference where you stand in the evolution discussion; the fact that humans are primates is not open for debate. So regardless of your ethnicity, primary language, or culture, you share about 95 percent of your DNA with chimps.

You also share a few other attributes. Whether we like it or not, many of our most basic drives mirror those of our hairy cousins. Chimps are social creatures living in small colonies with a distinct government. The arrangement seems very similar to a tribal human government. There is a ruling class not typically "elected," and the other members of the colony understand their place.

Chimps develop a rhythm to life that is based on deference. An alpha chimp is alpha in anything he chooses. Other chimps do not challenge his choice about which leaves will be good to nest in: If he is alpha, he can direct the group to nest in whatever leaves appeal to him. That primate behavior is just as prevalent in humans. Once someone proves herself more intelligent than you in accounting, she is likely going to get deference in other areas as well. It's reminiscent of the 1980's ad, "When E.F. Hutton speaks, people listen."

Think you're above that? Have you ever deferred to an actor for pain relief advice? Or to a musician for guidance on which candidate should sit in the White House? There is nothing fundamentally wrong with that model, because we are not cloistered. We have access to information about the same issues from other sources. They are only preying on our drives from a distance.

Morphing Behavior Standards

When humans are cloistered, and there is no mainstream outside influence to serve as a reminder of what's normal, then normal begins to look more and more like what is in the mind of those people on the bell curve who exceed what's normal—the people I call super-typicals. Sometimes this group image is distorted by forced deference such as violence or threats of violence, but more often it is distorted by human nature.

When collective thought begins to move in the direction of what is normal for the super-typical, he becomes even more of an authority. Wanting to be more like him, others in the group continually struggle to emulate the super-typical, whose behavior and tastes become the new standard. This action reflects the natural drive to differentiate the self from the group, and assert one's own distinction. The super-typical rewards this behavior—unless the acolyte attempts to bypass the master, in which case the upstart may find himself smacked down a rung on the status ladder. This progression toward the standard for the group is viewed as an accomplishment, and it leads directly to respect and a feeling of accomplishment.

This dynamic has played out in ugly ways in the context of the Iraq war, for example, with the abuse at Abu Ghraib being one of the most notorious. Nobody was around to watch as Charles Graner warped his team's sensibilities. Whatever he thought was fair treatment of prisoners became normal for the group. A little known fact is that all military police who guard prisoners are reservists. Why? We only need prison guards when we have a war. The by-product is that a group of schoolteachers, bank tellers, short-order cooks, and electricians may show up to guard prisoners. What if one of them is a penitentiary guard in his day job, as Graner was? Imagine the deference right out of the gate. Rank aside, he gains the role of informal leader.

The super-typical people can prey on the two fundamental drives—to belong and to differentiate—to get what they want. Many people are uncertain of where they belong in a group, or even *if* they belong, when in fact they are squarely typical. This can come from a bad or misshapen self-image, or simple insecurity that creates a distorted view, regardless of input from the outside. The super-typical helps them to feel needed or wanted, and thereby creates a sense of community. The stable, well-adjusted leader uses this to create a harmonious team; the unstable or demented leader creates an ever-morphing reality that progressively separates adherents from society. This negative use of positive tools was a primary mechanism for Charles Manson.

Some people barely clinging to sub-typical status within a group find other outlets to make themselves special. In order to differentiate, a person needs to belong. Because a person is not fully invested in his workplace group, for example, he finds belonging with another group and differentiates as much as he possibly can. Joe is a nobody at work, but he turns into the trivia champion of the local bar, or the best bowler at Victory Lanes. This differentiation may be much more important than anything at work—at least for now.

After reaching the pinnacle of success in an organization, people commonly look for peers somewhere else. Look around; how many successful people do you know who find pastimes to create a sense of belonging? In some cases, these people have differentiated themselves so much within the group that they are barely members, yet they stay where they are. They are so uncomfortable with leaving the small pond for fear of not being typical in a bigger pond that they stagnate. In the case of people such as Marshall Applewhite, the super-typical creates a new group, a place for the displaced to feel at home.

Putting the Dynamic to Work

You picked up this book to learn how to get others to do what you want, and what you know so far is that manipulating human behavior depends on understanding the human needs to belong and to differentiate.

Where do you fit on this continuum? Are you seeking belonging? Or does the need to differentiate outweigh it? Maybe you're above that on Maslow's pyramid of needs and your focus is self-actualization. In any case, your self-awareness will help you understand the dynamics of your own groups, and where the members sit on the bell curve. By analyzing the groups, you hone the analytical tools you need to examine groups of which you are not a member, as well as their members.

What you've also just learned through the examples I've cited is something about how influence is peddled. If the aberrant mind of a Jim Jones can convince others to do something horrendous with no master plan to guide the action, imagine how much simpler it should be for you to implement a plan for getting what you want.

Human Nature—the Trump Card

The Jim Jones example provides a perfect segue to another key group dynamic: fragmenting. It's a natural situation in which, even when a persuasive model is operating, the group splinters. The more complex the social dynamic, the tougher it is to make everyone understand where they belong. Some members become so distanced from the big fish that they begin to create subgroups with their own super-typical members. (This happens in companies all the time because the CEO or division head is inaccessible to most of the workers.) Although we will never know exactly what happened in Jonestown, we do know that the group fragmented. Allegations of abuse brought a member of the United States Congress to investigate, and the result was tragedy. If everyone in the Peoples Temple cult in Jonestown bought into Jones's thinking, then Congressman Leo Ryan would never have been murdered and 909 people would have died by their own hands—but they didn't. Many of them were also murdered for noncompliance or for acts that were overtly threatening to the cult.

Was it predictable? Fragmenting is always predictable. Whether you are chimp or a human, politics creates fracture. Primatologist Jane Goodall observed this kind of fracturing in her years with the chimps, too. Even in their relatively simple organizational structure, the chimps do not just fall into line and create an idyllic Kumbaya-style community with alpha benevolently ruling until death. As in the case of siblings Freud and Frodo, Freud ruled until he suffered from mange, and

Frodo overthrew him. Frodo ruled harshly, so as soon as he had a weak moment, he had to hide from the community that got tired of his ways. Sheldon moved in with his own power base and supplanted Frodo.

While humans may not be so overtly violent due to our larger and more evolved brains, we are proportionately more political, and our political games are just as dangerous. Some of the most savage politics in life revolve around a truly frustrated person who cannot achieve his true goals, and so he transfers all of that energy to a surrogate goal. That could range from a benign hobby to serial criminal acts.

In order to apply the skills associated with getting people to do what you want, you have to be able to predict the fracture points like this, and take advantage of them as well as know the dynamics of belonging and differentiating.

The Interrogation Link

Psychologically speaking, everyone has a part of him that needs to be touched. He may have close friends and family who know a great deal about him, but they don't know everything. If you, a perfect stranger, come along and trigger that person's need to expose a secret part of himself, he will tell you things he's never told anyone before.

Engaging a person's trust through body language, questioning in a way that leads him down a path of your design, and application of certain psychological levers will motivate that individual to bond with you.

That's the positive side. You offer him an opportunity.

On the negative side, you can use all of the same tools to engender a sense of helplessness, which is arguably an even more powerful emotion than trust or optimism.

As the American social philosopher Eric Hoffer (*The True Believer,* 1951) suggested, true believers take shape when they confront hopelessness and realize they have no option to improve their state unless they trust you (or in the case of religion, a pastor, rabbi, or other religious leader). The religious leader provides a model to which the fledgling believer cannot equal/compare, and then continues to pare options until the true believer emerges; that is, the person who embraces that the only path to success is the way of the leader. The wider the path, the narrower the gate.

Interrogators know this approach to motivation well. It's our secret weapon.

CHAPTER 2

The Dynamics in a Group

The sense of belonging and differentiating is *the* driver in every group, from the family unit to a major, multinational corporation. Companies rise or fall on the ability to exploit that fact, as do governments, churches, and other organizations. At the heart of when and how that sense of belonging occurs, or when and how that differentiation occurs, are the nature and style of a group's leadership.

Marketers: Masters of Belonging and Differentiating Others

I had a student once whose former wife had purchased tens of thousands of dollars worth of costume jewelry from QVC™—a fact he knew because they split up and had to declare their property. She had used her own money to make the purchases, so his concern wasn't that she had abused their joint accounts. His focus was on the weird sort of attachment she had to the QVC experience. "Why would she do that?" he asked me.

The reason is an essential factor in your getting people to do what you want: the need to belong. In a very short time, due to the ability of QVC employees to track customer purchases, when "Sally" would call to order, the people would talk to her as if they knew her. They were more like gals from the club than salespeople: "Good to talk to you! Where have you been, we missed you?" All true statements, but for dubious reasons. With Sally at home much of the time suffering from a debilitating disease, these sales pros were a main connection for conversation and caring. They gave her a genuine sense of belonging by knowing her, and they engendered her differentiation as she purchased more and more jewelry. When her name would pop up on the TV screen as having made a purchase, she would be acclaimed as "Sally, one of our favorite customers!"

I am not accusing QVC of predatory practices—I want to make that perfectly clear. These people simply do a good job of establishing a bond, a factor by which they can measure success. Once bonded, QVC employees help their best customers to feel differentiated. In part, eBay thrives because of the same psychology, by the way. You can quickly become a minor celebrity in the trading game, and you gain acknowledgement as such. You also get rah-rah e-mails that pronounce you a "winner" after making a successful purchase.

You're a winner because you competed against another person who had money to spend and you were able to spend more—now don't you feel great about that? Sure you do. You belong to an "exclusive" club of savvy bidders. You have what it takes to make eBay work for you.

BMW's longtime successful marketing strategy has been to link BMW ownership with identification to a particular social group. Aside from a brief foray into nonpremium territory, BMW has focused consistently on current customers who see themselves as privileged, and selecting new customers who want to belong to that group. In a manner that bears similarities to QVC, BMW went about forging an emotional bond with customers that relates to their belonging to the BMW family—a fact that automatically differentiates them from the unwashed masses. By the way, when I hear the term "family" used in relation to a product or group with whom I have no blood connection and only cursory ties, my Manson radar goes up.

Differentiating by Choice

To belong is the animal, to differentiate is the man. You can be differentiated from others in your group or society because you have talent, wealth, athleticism, and attractive features. All of those carry a positive connotation. But to be differentiated because you are weird is not a good thing unless you belong to a group of weirdoes. (Being eccentric among a group of eccentrics can make you super-typical.) People look at the lone oddball and wonder what else in going on in his head besides the bizarre stuff that just came out of his mouth.

Nevertheless, the need to differentiate is so strong that some people would rather go for the "crazy" label than the "ordinary" label. Many people also differentiate just by following their bliss, which may make them seem very odd in most contexts, but it just happens to give them a distinction they cherish. For example, I once worked with the director of operations for a construction company whose ability with needlepoint made him akin to daVinci with a bunch of thread. In fact, he had created a 3×4-foot needlepoint of daVinci's *Mona Lisa* that hung on the wall of his office. This 50-year-old family man by night, who controlled millions of dollars worth of construction projects by day, found needlepoint a relaxing, creative outlet. And it certainly made him different.

So where does normal stop and weird begin? It depends on what is normal for the group. Don't project your own values onto the group as you attempt to draw a member of the group closer to you.

The bottom line on differentiating might be summarized by an old joke. You don't have to outrun the bear, you just have to outrun your friend. In your group, you will likely have people who are smarter and faster than you. You just need to be smarter and faster than some. Smarter and faster are also relative terms. Those in your group may be the slowest and stupidest humans on the planet; that allows you to be smarter and faster in the cloistered group. Even if everyone in the group is smarter and faster than you are, you still have areas where you outstrip their performances. Most people are good at finding that on their own.

Mechanics of Manipulation

Bonding and fracturing are the operative concepts in making sure that the needs to belong and differentiate are met.

I want to clarify concepts here. The drivers are *belonging* and *differentiating*. The tools you use to prey on these most natural of human drives are *bonding* and *fracturing*. Think of it this way: Both of them function like a double-edged sword—cutting in both directions. This means each can potentially function in a positive or negative manner for positive or negative results. Fracturing can be applied to make someone stand out from the group when she is just a plain Jane, or to drive a wedge between her and the group and create a need to draw closer to the group or someone else. Bonding can be used to bring the person who is feeling isolated into a group, or to take the alpha down a notch to a plain old monkey.

Look at one scenario of how someone can manage another person's journey along Maslow's Hierarchy of Needs. I'll use a Charles Manson–like example because his notorious story is so well known.

Our leader finds a young woman who is different from those around her, someone who feels like an outsider. He establishes a place of belonging so that she feels nurtured, safe, and protected. The insulation allows him to drive new "family" ideas into her head and to show her "the way"—the way to belonging; self-esteem; and, ultimately, self-actualization. This act of bonding her more closely to the family's ideals and making her feel as though she has a place in the group is a fracturing action to take her away from mainstream connections. As she begins to understand how she fits and she adopts the family rules, she wants to be more like the leader (the super-typical). The leader sets the rules. Using his own leadership style, he informs everyone else how they measure up. When our subject starts to emulate the leader, she is attempting to differentiate just like a Boy Scout earning merit badges; she is living up to the standards that her group espouses. If she gets to a point where the leader fears he will lose control of her, he simply over-differentiates, and she starts to fracture from the group. And then she feels the need to belong creeping back in. In effect, what he has done is drop her back to the "belonging" tier of Maslow's Hierarchy.

Before you can say LaBianca-Tate Murders, our subject is so bonded to the groupthink that she does not remember how the outside world functions. She, similar to the young soldier I described in Chapter 1, is getting all the self-image input she needs from those who understand "the way." Only if and when she breaks from the group and starts to get new inputs and new standards by which to live does she consider that there was a problem. She may even say things such as, "He was perfect. Divine." In fact, it was more than a description of exaggerated praise. The filter embedded in her by the group gave her such a distorted self-image that she truly believed he was divine and perfect—the light and the way. The result was a person who would do anything to achieve this perfection.

Voluntary and Involuntary Bonding

The only truly natural bond you have in life is blood. When you are born to a line of people, like it or not, you have a bond you cannot sever. You can choose never to speak, to see, or to think about that group again; but oddly enough, that very group will have an effect on your thoughts, actions, and responses, regardless of whether you leave before you can crawl. That is, because you have the same DNA, you share the operating system that your blood relations have. You may reprogram and fine-tune, but your new upgrades are still running on, and on top of, the same hardware and operating system as the rest of your family. It is fairly easy (and convenient) to reject this assertion when you're a kid, but you can't do it credibly when you're older because, as we age, we see more and more of our birth parents in the mirror. Many mannerisms, and even many thoughts, may be rooted in the biology, rather than the nurturing, we receive. You can walk away from all other organizations and erase all memory of the association.

If this sounds like too extreme an assertion, consider this story of a personal friend of Maryann's. "Charly" grew up in a very happy, conventional family in the Pittsburgh area. Her little sisters were cheerleaders who married right out of high school. She was the studious one. Mom and Dad doted on their first-born, but never connected with her academic aspirations all that well. Charly got her PhD in English literature and taught at a major university, and she spent the next 20 years developing her career. One day, she got the call that her father had died. When she sat at a table at the wake with her parents' long-time neighbor, she thought she was looking in the mirror. Her sisters never needed glasses, but Charly had thick ones—like the neighbor. Her sisters were blonde. She was brunette—like the neighbor. Her sisters didn't like school. But Charly, similar to the neighbor, had pursued a PhD in spite of the family's obvious disinterest. They were both lefties, too. According to Charly, she said something like, "My father didn't die, did he?" And the answer was, "No. I'm still here."

So when I say that the family is the only natural, or involuntary, group that occurs, I'm referring to a genetic link. For some of you, that surviving, natural group comprises only two people who are blood relatives, such as siblings, mom and child, and father and child. I contrast that unit with artificial organizations—and I use this word without prejudice to refer to businesses, churches, clubs, or any other groups not composed strictly of blood relatives—in which people come together for common purposes and interests, rather than just because they share DNA.

Think about that concept of artificial organizations as you wind your way through life. Look at how much you try to be more like the groups you voluntarily join. More importantly, look in the mirror and consider how much effort you make to differentiate yourself from the group to which you cannot help but belong—your family.

In some cases, we want so badly for our family to be more, that we try to differentiate the whole family. As we amass a fortune, distinguish ourselves academically, win a gold medal, or otherwise pull ourselves up by the bootstraps, we try to become a surrogate for the entire family as we differentiate our way through society.

The dynamic of family is hard to overstate. When people think of ties that cannot be broken, these ties often prey on the model of family. Looking at Charles Manson once again, consider how he took people who had fled their families for one reason or another, and created a nucleus to which each felt drawn at a primal level. He called this group "the family." Manson used his personality (quirky as it is), age differential, and prior run-ins with "the man" to show his value and establish himself as leader of this group.

Each group, whether family or other, will establish leadership in a distinctive way, which is often determined by the dynamic that causes the core group to come into existence in the first place. For example, if a charismatic individual magnetically draws needy people to him, the dynamic takes shape from the moment of recruitment. Different organizational dynamics related to bonding and fragmenting emerge depending on the group's leadership factors: selection method, strength of the leader, the leader's style of influence, and the impact of isolation.

Natural Versus Imposed Leaders, or How a Leader Ascends to Power

All groups have a leader, whether that person is sanctioned by a formal process or simply emerges in a position of authority.

The simplest kind of leader is the guy in the office who steps up to solve a problem; this guy is a natural or informal leader. He may invite himself to seize power or simply respond to cries for help. In either case, there is no deliberate, delineated process, and there are no formal trappings of authority. He may get deference from everyone in the office, or simply be viewed as an oaf who is stuck with the role in the beginning, but given enough time he will gain real power and deference. The key point is, he is there to represent and make decisions, sometimes through openly exercising authority, and other times through less overt wrangling.

Informal, or *natural,* leaders emerge in response to a power vacuum, whether or not the vacuum is evident. An example on the whimsical side is the guy who organizes the annual football pool at the office; a more practical example is the person who speaks up for his coworkers in front of the boss. The social version is the neighbor who arranges the holiday parties and organizes everyone against a new mega-store. The neighborhood or other nonwork-related leaders are the kinds of informal leaders who get harder to avoid. You can change jobs, but changing neighborhoods for most people is a bit more traumatic.

Informal leaders have just as much authority as though they were appointed by a king or elected overwhelmingly by the populace. Oprah Winfrey exemplifies this kind of leader, who has the power to command attention whenever she wants it and to influence significant decisions in peoples' lives. If you have someone in the workplace who stands out as this kind of informal leader, the boss knows that deference is in order. I have been in many work environments where it was clear that the man with the title was not the man with the power.

The second type of leader is *formal*, or *imposed*. The underpinning of formality is a recognized process to select the leader who then fills an official slot and carries the crown and scepter of the position. I describe this leader as imposed because, in most cases, not everyone has a say in who gets the role. When the board of directors hires your new boss, you likely have little input in the decision. His leadership is imposed and, although you can opt to leave, that is likely as much power as you can exercise. At the same time, it doesn't mean that simply reminding people of his status will enable him to accomplish anything.

When I was a very young soldier, my first job was as a finance clerk—something for which I was not suited at all. My boss was a 22-year-old lieutenant who had a horrible management style. He would come into our office, cross his arms, walk around, and watch us work. It was like a caricature from a Monty Python movie. After one of the guys who worked in our office died in a car crash, people really started to bond against the lieutenant. The sense was, "What if this is me tomorrow? I shouldn't have to put up with this crap." So a few days later, in an effort to improve morale, the lieutenant decided to bring himself down to the level of his minions. He closed the door and said, "All rank's off. I want you guys to be point-blank honest with me. How do you feel?" The words were barely out of his mouth when a young woman nearly spat out, "You're an ignorant mother—." What went through my mind, with more than a little amusement, was "That was the wrong thing to say, young lieutenant. You should have laid some ground rules." What he was trying to do was bond, but instead he fractured very quickly. He was put in power because the establishment ordained him, not because he had any competence in the areas of people management or finance. Merely because he was in charge, he thought he had power. In truth, he had no power to make anyone do what he wanted. He never asked for or earned authority from the people he was governing.

You might conclude that, because this was the military, a certain amount of deference had to be given to someone who outranks you. True, but you can provide formal deference to a formal leader and it rings hollow. This lieutenant, in effect, removed the veil, and saw clearly that he could make people do what he said, but never what he wanted. The young lieutenant asked for a transfer.

The army learned from this fiasco, and replaced the lieutenant with a seasoned sergeant who had done the jobs of the people sitting in the office. He got cooperation and respect as soon as he demonstrated the understanding borne of that experience. His opening remarks communicated the message, "Give me permission to help you," and that gave people in the office the opening they needed to find reasons to respect him.

Years later, I encountered a management situation in which the department head was despised by eight of her employees, got along marginally with one, and was friends with another.

The CEO would not get rid of her, however, because she had built strong relationships with some powerful clients. The one person with whom she got along marginally well took charge as the informal leader and served as the go-between for the employees who hated their boss. She carried requests from them to the boss, and transmitted orders and answers back to them from the boss. This is how she kept the department intact—with the loss of only one staff member—for two years. After the boss left of her own accord, the go-between assumed leadership of the department.

Some idealistic people who were born yesterday (not you) would assert that the freely elected presidents of the United States are formal leaders, but not imposed. Dwell on that idea for just a few minutes. The president of the United States is imposed on many who disagree with that person being president. Majority rules, so he is a leader imposed on the minority. In some practical ways, many members of Congress serve the same function as the woman who acted as go-between in her department—shuttling demands between their constituents who don't like the current administration, and the current administration who thinks, "I'm in the big house now. You have to do it my way."

A natural leader can quickly become a formal leader. A historically positive example is George Washington. Through the use of charisma, or just plain people skills, the natural leader can become the obvious selection for the formal leader. Similar to the informal leader who replaced the department manager, sometimes stepping up leads to formal authority.

Throughout history, there are also terrific examples of this, such as Adolph Hitler and Charles Manson.

These are two very different models for informal leaders seizing power. In one case, an informal leader uses his physical or intellectual appeal and charisma to get others to see things his way. In fact, through demonstrating his sexual prowess and natural hatred for "the man," Manson established himself as the *informal* leader of his cult-like group. Oddly enough, in a group of antiestablishment malcontents, the fact that Manson had been incarcerated made him super-typical rather than sub-typical. As the group became more and more established as the Manson Family, he became the de facto leader, therefore, he became formally in charge.

In the other case, Hitler forged connections through his natural leadership and rose to power in an insulated group, and then leveraged his power base to national authority. Similar to Manson, Hitler had spent time in prison for opposing "the man." In the end, the leverage and cult of personality gained him a position of authority in the formal and imposed leadership of the country. With a few very Machiavellian moves, Hitler seized power.

Hitler and Manson are people who understood the power of informal leadership and influence, and who used that voluntary surrendering of authority as a foot in the door to ask for, and get, absolute power over others' lives. In some cases, the request centered on using the absolute authority granted by a small group to enforce authority over a larger group. In either case the informal morphed into formal and imposed.

A leader can also be a formal, imposed leader who has the trust and sway with the people to whom others would listen even if he were not imposed. These personalities come along once in awhile in politics, and quickly achieve almost legendary status for their impact. Whether you liked their views or not, few people can argue with the persuasive power that Ronald Reagan and Bill Clinton held. These two men held the public's attention through two very different styles, but for the same reason: personality. Both had their trials with political opponents and their followers, but both survived and were reelected by electoral majority, and continued to flourish in arguably the most difficult job in the world.

People in everyday life use this same skill set. Whether imposed or informal leaders, many people will create a cult of personality and use the seemingly inconspicuous opportunity as a means to gain increasing levels of authority over others. There is an adage that few people ever surrender power, so be very careful to whom you surrender yours.

Strong or Weak

Because assessing the strength or weakness of leadership relies on an analog view and not a binary one, the concept of either/or does not fit perfectly here. A leader's style falls somewhere on a scale between lifeless and Draconian. Most leaders—at least most who stay around for awhile—find a style that occupies the middle ground.

Regardless of how the leader rises to power, strength of leadership plays a role in his success. While difficult for the informal leader to seize all power immediately, it is not impossible. An informal leader can use sleight of hand or even overt techniques to capture power from those below and above him in the hierarchy. Depending on personal agenda, the informal leader may truly only want to represent his people, and will rein himself in accordingly, or he may see the opportunity to become a de facto ruler. In the latter case, he simply leverages the power base he has created with those he is "helping" to show that he is a factor that cannot be overlooked. Hitler used this to great effect in his rise to power. Once the informal leader begins to get the power base established with those above him, the power he wields over those he represents becomes more formalized. Regardless of whether the leader is formal or informal, the personality of the leader will affect how he wields this new power. The informal leader has to walk a fine line: Exercise too much authority, and he will be ousted. Too little, and he will be ineffective. Because the skill set to be an effective informal leader is so complex, those who master it are often recognized for their prowess and become formal leaders as a matter of natural progression.

While informal leaders may be in the role for the fun of it, most formal leaders are in it for gain, whether financial or esteem. This means they have more at stake than most informal leaders. Often people say "the power has gone to his head," but the core truth to which that statement points is much more insidious. When a person has more at stake, stress rises. Stress changes the personality style of many people, and they go to what has worked in the past, either for them or for one of their role models. In many cases, the skill set is the one that worked for the person in an informal role, or a formal role in a smaller pond, and it is ineffective in the current role. The result is an extreme reaction as the person panics and starts to try to gain equilibrium. The leader may be paralyzed by the options and incapable of flexing any strength, or he may simply panic and respond with overwhelming force, depending on his personality.

Often, very weak formal leadership will result in "armed" camps within an organization as factions form along invisible lines and natural leaders stake their claims. I was once part of an army unit afflicted by a tremendous amount of infighting. Our leadership was located remotely from the working location of the unit and, due to our mission, rarely saw their troops. The unit was a blend between combat arms soldiers and interrogators—oil and water. The combat arms troops functioned quite well with little to no supervision and weak central leadership. Not long after 20 interrogators joined the unit, however, the disintegration started. Most people in the group were the same rank, or very close to it, but there were also imposed leaders who outranked the masses. These people were from both the combat arms and interrogation groups as well. Although the soldiers did what they were ordered to do, that is all they did. When the leaders' intent was "x," but he inadvertently communicated "x minus," the soldiers played barracks lawyers and interpreted the order in such a way that they disobeyed the intent of the order. The unit fragmented. The lines were drawn between "the interrogator folks" and "the combat arms folks." A third group—"the others"—were assorted folks not clearly identified with either of the warring factions. Having been in infantry battalions before and changing jobs to become an interrogator, I identified more with the combat arms group.

Most interrogators considered themselves superior for the mission, as did most combat arms folks. The pressure to side with one or the other was pervasive, but not overt. The result was chaos and infighting at every turn.

When the new commander came in, he clearly saw the issue. In an afternoon conversation, he asked me how I thought I could draw warring factions together. I told him I believed a common enemy was the best amalgamator. He took my words to heart as he created a Draconian style that caused all groups to hate him and unite for a common cause—a noble and dangerous action on his part, and it worked. He understood that his imposed status insulated him from retribution in that setting, so he forged ahead, arrogantly proclaiming what he meant and how he meant it. Unlike the junior lieutenant who managed the cadre of finance clerks, this officer never allowed his subordinates to rise up. In this way, he replaced weak central leadership with iron-fisted browbeating.

Consider how the fragmentation could occur in a neighborhood without a strong, natural, or imposed leader. Most residents are longtime members of a neighborhood composed of 1950s style split-level houses, and life has worked into a natural rhythm. While there are natural leaders for things such as standard of living and decoration, the group has no need for a strong leader. A new couple moves in from an artistic community in the mountains and quickly decides to dress up their new place with some color. After a few coats of primary colors on the old house, the new residents are ecstatic. They assume their new neighbors will find the splits of the house—blue, yellow, and red—a fun way to modernize an old design.

While trying to settle in, the new couple passes out flyers inviting their new neighbors to a party. A few people show up, but the majority does not. Among those that show are a couple who think the idea is great, but would never do it themselves; a few others who are indifferent to the radical change; and finally, a vocal antagonist. Rising up to his role as natural leader, he takes it upon himself to ask them what the hell is going on. The neighborhood spins out of control.

Many neighborhood covenants have sprung up to prevent this exact form of chaos. But what happens when a Draconian-style, cult-leader wannabe steps up, as in this case? A kind of police state for a neighborhood. Tony from the corner lot is informally elected to be the neighborhood covenant officer. Tony makes it his crusade to interpret the rules and ensure everyone in the neighborhood hides the air-conditioning units outside the house with shrubbery, and he harasses neighbors who leave garden hoses out. Tony is overboard in flexing his muscles, and differentiates at home because he is a nobody at work. The level of anxiety and frustration causes the neighbors to unite and remove Tony from his post as the enforcer of neighborhood covenants. Unlike the military commander, Tony is imposed, but only for as long as his constituents are willing to tolerate his zealotry. There is a difference between a strong leader and an obnoxious, pushy one.

The best indicator that you have weak leadership is infighting. No one has had the ability or vision to establish a common cause or a common enemy. Chimps in a tribe will beat each other up on a regular basis, but as soon as a chimp from a rival tribe shows up, all the focus is on beating him up. A strong leader finds a way to spotlight the foreign "chimp." Draconian leaders have a tendency to become a common enemy for the group and drive a more cohesive team. The downside is that the parties at war will only stop fighting for one purpose: to sabotage that enemy.

Neither of these styles is impervious to the cult of personality that can evolve in a vacuum, and both extremes have a tendency to create fractures. The Draconian leaders' fractures just take longer to show up. Either leadership style lends itself to being usurped, as well as informal leaders with Machiavellian intent.

Unless you were a feral child, you have had imposed leaders at least until you were old enough to choose. In two-parent families, one is often the disciplinarian (translate: Draconian leader) while the other is the pushover—or so it appears. The division of authority that goes on between the parents in healthy households is a good example of power-sharing and using the dynamic of each other's strength.

In some cases the imposed leader will unwittingly, or even knowingly, give his authority to someone else who is a natural leader and a more forceful personality. This kind of transfer of power goes on in all kinds of organizations from the smallest to the largest.

Even in a family of two, you can have both types of leaders. A smart, rational teenager in a house full of distracted adults and rambling toddlers could emerge as the informal leader. I know a home where that happened. Through inaction due to paralysis caused by dealing with other issues, the parent surrenders authority to the adolescent. Or worse, a strong natural leader personality emerges in the child of a parent who finds it amusing, but does not know how to handle the precocious little bundle of joy. The next thing you know the parent is in the role of tender to the ego of the child.

In artificial groups such as the workplace, most people have to deal with an alpha whom they did not select and over whom they have no control. These alphas were not elected—the boss, the Pope, or the commanding officer—but each one has an unnatural amount of authority that is hard to supplant. Here, too, the natural leader may usurp authority and begin to hold court by getting the blessing of the appointed alphas and, to use an army term, "wearing their stripes."

The United States military offers an undeniable illustration of this kind of behavior. Army wives often assume the rank of their husbands. The wife of an officer, for example, may treat the husband's subordinates as if they are her own. Worse yet, she may try to manage the wives of her husband's subordinates as if they were her subordinates. This creates some unusual and complex dynamics, both in the workplace and in social settings.

When a unit commander is strong in his leadership style at work, but not so in charge at home, the dynamic can destroy an otherwise cohesive unit. Morale plummets.

Styles of Influence

There are no simple criteria for what is a good leadership style. In my mind, the only criterion is effectiveness. What I have seen work in the military has varied. Some leaders are father figures, others manipulative. Yet others distinguish themselves through coalition building.

Authoritarian Versus Democratic

In simple terms, this is *telling* versus *asking*. "Telling" may sound a lot like strength, but it is not necessarily the style of choice for a strong leader. Some Draconian managers routinely ask people to do what they want—"How would you like to take on an extra territory?"—and in the process create a tremendous following by getting positive outcomes. At the same time, they disenfranchise those who do not succeed in that system. In my personal experience with someone like this, when someone failed to comply with the manager's request, she not only expressed her disappointment in a swift and severe fashion, she also created an environment where the person was ostracized. The effect of asking is that people often feel obligated on a much higher level than when the leader tells them what to do. The leader who asks is tying the outcome of the group to the request and creating a feeling of tribal obligation. That can be one of the strongest leadership tactics anyone can exercise.

Open Versus Maneuvering

Effective leaders can be open and straightforward, or maneuvering like a snake in the grass and difficult to discern. Consider these two styles of leadership influence and think of the variations on them.

1. **Aboveboard.** Whether authoritarian or democratic, this style of leader asks for what she wants up front. She may be a strong or weak personality, but it is clear in her expectations of others. The benefit to this style is that people know where they stand and situations rarely explode. The disadvantage is that it creates a lot of hidden intrigue, because people under the leader try to find ways to counter her effectiveness. The key to dealing with her lies is to understand that just because she tells you what she wants tactically does not mean she is divulging what she is trying to accomplish strategically. She is still capable of having a grand scheme that is impossible to discern. She simply does not use subterfuge to get it. She asks openly and receives each step in her master plan.

2. **Chess-playing.** To this kind of leader, whether you are a subordinate or a peer, you are a piece on the board. The wise chess player understands that anyone can serve the function of an ill-placed pawn or have the killing strength of a queen. The

chess player may tell some people his plan, but use others as a blocking mechanism to set up his next move. The chess player needs to insulate himself with valuable pieces to protect himself. The danger is that a pawn catches on, or a valued member of the inner sanctum is sacrificed. The chess player's approach to the game often fails dramatically. To be effective, chess players need a fair amount of charisma or clout, or both.

A broad band of possibilities exists in addition to these two. Consider the variations with just the chess player: he may be an aggressive leader who takes bold risks, or he will differ from the spineless chess player who sacrifices pieces timidly. The method of his rise to power will also dictate behaviors: did people around him laud his methods, or did he talk his way into the game?

Liabilities haunt both of the extremes of the chess player. The aggressive leader who uses his subordinates to lay a minefield for those who oppose him will probably be very effective until those subordinates have a crisis of faith: "Tell me again; why am I doing this?" And the timid leader who arranges to have his subordinates sacrificed will have hell to pay if he doesn't have a moral imperative and a decisive victory. In both cases, the perception of subterfuge can doom them.

The crisis of faith will occur quickly for the above-board leader when those who have come to trust him for his honesty discover he has been hiding his agenda in plain sight. While the leader may not be hiding anything deliberately, his followers simply may have misunderstood the long-term objective or blinded themselves to the obvious. The most disillusioning turn of events in life can be the discovery that you have voluntarily followed someone to an end you did not predict. This sudden understanding of your own frailty can result in a tremendous backlash to the aboveboard leader.

What is your style, and to what style do you respond? In order to design a plan to get what you want, you need to understand how leaders motivate you to perform and what range of styles you can use to motivate others. In any case, both formal and informal leadership grant the leader a type of super-typical status if the person is effective in that role.

Isolation as a Tactic of Leadership

A community with no external influences, or communication with the outside world that is funneled through a controlling source, will become cloistered. As illustrated by Zimbardo's Stanford prison experiment described in Chapter 1, the impact of that cloistering on behavior is potentially shocking. Whether formal or informal, the leader becomes the absolute authority for the group, the members of which seek his approval.

If an informal leader seizes power abruptly, the result is likely displacement; the formal leader will see a mass exodus. Germany's wartime and post-wartime brain drain in the mid-20th century provides an example of the latter. Maryann participated in such an exodus from a theater company for which she worked, where the board of directors hastily decided to put salaries for staff and actors on hold until the season subscription money came in. Not only was it an illegal move ("there's always unemployment compensation…"), but also disrespectful enough to cause six of 10 staff members to leave just as hastily as the board had made their decision.

An extremely charismatic leader may be able to fend off the inevitable a bit longer than others, but the issue becomes not "if" but "when." If he can hold them long enough to initiate a transformation of the standards of the group, fracturing from societal norms is bound to happen. If he cannot, then his attempt fails.

Given enough time, even if the leader is not particularly charismatic, he may be able to effect a turnaround by appealing to collective beliefs and altering them to play on groupthink in creating a cult of personality, that is, he alters the collective consciousness of the group. This is the kind of phenomenon that has happened in congregations that splinter from the larger church community: as they bind closer to the pastor's pattern of thinking, they grow more critical of the policies and practices of the umbrella organization.

With the needs of belonging and differentiating shaping so many of our decisions as humans, we have a duty to ourselves to pay attention to the people in our lives who have the potential to satisfy those needs. On a grand scale, they are the imposed leaders of our companies and government. But the people who enforce neighborhood covenants or seize power at the Rotary Club meeting can have just as much impact—or more—on the sense of well-being associated with our getting those needs met. Start asking yourself: What is the reason he has so much sway over me? Is he exercising authority that has been given to him, or am I surrendering authority? Is he really charismatic, or am I perceiving him as charismatic due to circumstances? If you are the one in power, pay attention to the dynamic and polish your skills. If you are not formally in power, map the dynamic and use it to polish others' perception of you.

CHAPTER 3

Mechanics of Charisma

Humans often overlook the most obvious things about other humans—and I start with myself in making that judgment. As a student of human behavior, I am much like Jane Goodall among the chimps, with one exception: I am also a chimp. So even though I know a fair amount about people, I can overlook basic things because I am caught up in the interplay that is humanity.

When average people run into a highly charismatic person, what is it that they recall about the person? Everyone who has an encounter with a decidedly charismatic person recounts the story in very similar fashion, regardless of whether the encounter went well or ended in tragedy. Whether it was, "He made me feel as though I was the only person in the room," or "He made me feel as though he was divine," it is always about a *feeling* and not facts.

Followers of Charles Manson, David Koresh, and many other leaders of both cults and genuine religious sects have described *their* leaders as gods or godlike, just like this man who followed the Maharaji: "I believed he was the living incarnation of God," said Joe Whalen in his posting on the *www.ex-premie.org* Website. And then, he went on to describe his feelings in detail: "...when I was allowed to enter the ashram, I was happy, excited, and I felt privileged for the opportunity he, the Perfect Master, gave me."

I considered all of the cult leaders and how each has been described as charismatic. After I looked at Koresh, with his obvious facial display of emotional disturbance, Manson the raging madman, the paranoid Jim Jones, and Marshall Applewhite—who met the "Bo" half of his Bo-Peep cult leadership in a Houston psychiatric hospital—I asked myself again how is it that these people could be perceived as charismatic. Is there a skill set they were applying? Can it be codified? Is this intentional? Chemical? I also started to look for a good definition of the word *charismatic*.

Go straight to the dictionary definition of charisma. The Merriam-Website online dictionary calls it "a special magnetic charm or appeal."

The Wikipedia entry on charisma suggests charisma is a bit of snake oil. It reads as follows:

Though very difficult or even impossible to define accurately (due to a lack of widely accepted criteria in regard to the trait), charisma is often used to describe an elusive, even indefinable personality trait that often includes the seemingly "supernatural" or uncanny ability to lead, charm, persuade, inspire, and/or influence people.

Notably neither entry says anything about being born with it, although you might have been.

So here again is the inherently illogical challenge. How do you study the magic someone is using while you are under his spell? The answer is likely something akin to Arthur C. Clarke's magic theorem: any sufficiently advanced technology is indistinguishable from magic.

What I did was take as many steps back as I could from charisma and analyze it. My conclusion is that it is more technique than magic.

Because charisma is "impossible to define," and always referred to in terms of feelings, my inquisitive nature sought to define it in logical terms. I began with the premise that, if you cannot define something, then how do you know it exists? It's real if you can see the effect of it. The effect in this case is a feeling. Accepting it as proof that the elusive character trait exists, the next step is to look at it like all other human traits: as a process or series of processes.

All good interrogators know that feelings can be created and managed through definable processes; therefore, charisma is a flavor of manipulation. Not always intentional, this is one process rarely understood by the wielder, which is no doubt part of why it seems shrouded in mystery.

Time to remove the shroud. I call this process that leaves a discernable mark or pattern of responses the "mechanics of charisma."

I believe that charisma can be defined, and is explainable rather than elusive. What I do agree with is that it carries the aura of otherworldly abilities. Now it's your turn to acquire them.

If you do not see yourself as particularly charismatic, here are the steps to change that. If you do, here is your path to intensifying your natural magnetism and understanding how others use charisma on you. The five steps are:

1. Demonstrate value.
2. Recognize opportunity.
3. Grant an audience.
4. Create belonging.
5. Differentiate your target.

Step 1: Demonstrate Value

In 1974, Donald G. Dutton and Arthur P. Aron of the University of British Columbia published the results of a study citing the probable link between a sense of danger and sexual arousal ("Some Evidence for Heightened Sexual Attraction under Conditions of High Anxiety," *Journal of Personality and Social Psychology*, 1974, Vol. 30, No. 4, 510–517). The gist is that men on a shaky suspension bridge swaying over a 200-foot drop had a stronger sexual response to an attractive female researcher on the bridge than did the men on a stable, conventional bridge.

To these men in the study, she had a lot of magnetism. Why? First of all, the woman on the bridge demonstrated value by virtue of being:

1. **Attractive.** If you compare her to Miss (name the month) in *Playboy*, she was not in the same league. But she came across as much more attractive than she would have been on a crowded New York street because she was seen in isolation. The men on the bridge with heightened awareness had no one to whom they could compare her.

2. **Unusual.** Here was an attractive woman—and I'm using the definition constructed previously—on an ostensibly dangerous, swinging bridge. If you're a man, think of how many times you have encountered an attractive woman at a moment when you thought you were about to plunge 200 feet into a rocky gorge?

3. **Intelligent.** She took each man she encountered through a questionnaire pertaining to psychological research. You may not think that's sexy, but it certainly adds an intriguing dimension to the package.

Although the experiment was designed to show heightened sexual arousal, a similar study about charisma would likely have the same result. The combination of factors differentiated the young survey-taker from the men. In most cases, being physically attractive is enough of a differentiator, but add the other factors to that, and she was suddenly dramatically different in several ways.

You may not have the ability to use as many factors to create an image of differentiation strong enough that your audience wants to know more. More likely, you will be able to demonstrate value to your audience through some kind of single stimulus. It could be as simple as wearing something odd that distinguishes you from other people and draws their attention to you, but if your intended audience sees that as having entertainment value, for example, it is still a demonstration of value.

When I interrogated Arab-speaking prisoners I had a clear path to demonstrate value. I must have been valuable because he was required to talk to me, and because I was likely one of the few Americans around who spoke his language. Even then, my demeanor and skill set as I went about establishing rapport and questioning him needed to illustrate value constantly. If I walked into the room and instantly let him know exactly what I was thinking, what I knew, and what I needed to know, as well as my plan for getting him to talk, I would be nothing more than another piece of furniture in the room. My source needed to feel as though my opinion mattered and I had compelling reasons to ask him questions about himself in addition to questions about his activities.

Think of this value in terms of credibility. George Piro, an FBI field agent, recently disclosed on *60 Minutes* that he interrogated Saddam Hussein five to seven hours per day for four months without ever disclosing he was only a field agent. He allowed Saddam to believe he was a high-level official answering to the president of the United States to maintain credibility. In effect, by playing on Saddam's ego, he enhanced his value to Saddam.

This demonstration of value has to be one that maintains a veil around you. If you have nothing but one card trick to offer, and you quickly divulge that fact, you have missed your opportunity to convey value. However, if you can maintain a flirtatious fan-dance approach that hides your many tricks, you have effectively created value. You need to create an image, which may be based on many components, that is sustainable for the duration of the time you want to maintain your charismatic effect.

Life offers many opportunities for differentiation. Different things impact different people, so your tactic has to take into account your target audience. In the 1960s, a woman not wearing something (such as a bra), had more than entertainment value—it was a political statement that differentiated her. Depending on her audience, that could have been taken as a differentiator that drew people to her for her courage, or simply despised her for her lack of morals. It takes a certain amount of confidence to have that kind of presence, but there are many other ways compatible with a more reticent persona that you can use to differentiate yourself from the crowd. All have one thing in common: you show you are something other than the norm.

Humor is a great differentiator if you are genuinely funny and able use some generic principles, such as pointing out the incongruity in a common situation, to get a laugh. In contrast to that, the humor in a joke is usually a subjective call.

Some obvious differentiators are physical attributes, such as beauty, grace, speed, and height; others are clothing, or the lack thereof. Just remember your target audience; wearing hooker clothes to church will differentiate you, but playing the organ on short notice will get a warmer reception.

The value you create should mark you as above the other person's station. This does not mean you actually are above the other person. The key is perception. Because of how you demonstrated value, that individual sees you as somehow above him.

Right after basic training, I was reassigned to a new base for job-specific training. When I arrived, a young soldier who was only slightly ahead of me in his career gave presentations to all soldiers en route to the fort. This payroll guy helped soldiers fill out forms and understood how everyone got paid. He stood in front of a room full of both recruits and officers. Anyone who wanted to get paid had to be in the briefing. I couldn't stand the sight of this guy; he had acne so bad it looked like someone had tried to put out a fire with an ice pick on his face. But he did what he did better than anyone else, and that made him a local celebrity—someone differentiated from the rest of us. Even people who outranked him sought him out and wanted to listen to what he had to say. He was swarmed with people talking to him not only about pay, but just conversation in general. The mere fact that he was the face of the finance team and delivering this briefing on a daily basis to many people distinguished him.

EXERCISE: HAVE, DO, KNOW

Make a list of things you do that other people don't do, things you have that other people don't have, and people that you have met or know well—celebrities of one sort or another—who most people do not. Don't overshoot. Make choices that have roots in fact and verifiable experience. Maybe you are the good presenter or the guy who has the best stories. That means you've conquered Step 1. Start to think of this as a stock: something that gives you leverage and possibilities.

Move this concept closer to home. The guy in the next cubicle who understands how to deliver a powerful presentation gets adulation and admiration from others in the office. Often, he brushes it aside without regard for the implications and possibilities. He misses the opportunity to exploit the differentiator, because he sees himself as a known quantity who has shown all his cards already.

This self-effacing conclusion should remind you of your own experiences with teachers, coaches, and bosses who had no idea how much sway they held over their charges. How many of you had a crush on a teacher or professor, and then later matured and wondered, "What was I thinking?" Maryann admits that, after four years of female teachers, she had a gigantic crush on her 5th-grade teacher, and thought that he was the handsomest man alive. When she saw a picture in the newspaper of his fiancée, she was confused. This was not the stunning beauty that should beat her out of the chance to have his undying affection.

The initial reaction—something that approaches adoration—reflects that part of the human psyche that manufactures charisma. Value is in the eyes of the beholder.

In *The Game* (William Morrow, 2005), Neil Strauss recounts the secrets of manipulation he learned during an extended foray into the world of pick-up artists. His mentor, Mystery, counseled him to effect what I call differentiation; here's Strauss's description of his early efforts:

> I wore stylish jackets with bright shirts and accessorized as much as I could. I bought rings, a necklace, and fake piercings. I experimented with cowboy hats, feather boas, light-up necklaces, and even sunglasses at night to see which received the most attention from women. In my heart, I knew most of these gaudy accouterments were tacky, but Mystery's peacock theory worked. When I wore at least one item that stood out, women who were interested in me had an easy way to start a conversation.

Strauss's experience is the beginning of having a charismatic effect on someone: getting the person's attention.

Keep in mind that the central element of your success is that you need to offer something that gives the other person a feeling that you are both differentiated and you have real value.

Some factors occur naturally, such as good looks or other striking physical attributes. Others are cultivated, such as a tremendous vocabulary, a wonderful speaking voice, or rapier wit. Still others require contrivance to establish your value, such as the peacock theory that Strauss's mentor Mystery advocates. I listed these here in order of preference. If you happen to be gifted from birth, you have an unfair advantage. But do not dismay if you were born average—simply cultivate a skill. Too late, you say? You need this now? Then go to the third option: contrive something. A feather boa may not work for you, but find something you can carry off that gives you the opportunity for which you are looking.

EXERCISE: DEMONSTRATE VALUE

Experiment with how easy it is to catch and hold someone's attention by demonstrating value. The site could be your office, a party, or any other setting where you know in advance you will be with people. Hang something you made or acquired on the wall of your office. Or wear a pink feather in your hair to the party, unless you look like me, in which case that would be too strange for words. Just do or say something compatible with your personality and experiences that sets you apart, and let it do the work of drawing someone closer to you.

Consider these variables in choosing how to demonstrate value:

1. **Audience receptivity.** Being the best hip-hop dancer in a biker gang may not be what you're after. If you differentiate toward the weird at a science fiction convention, you might be okay, but walking into a business meeting wearing red contact lenses is likely not the right answer.

2. **Snowball effect/groupthink.** This describes a phenomenon of influence that is most likely to occur when your audience is isolated, at least to some degree. Remember that self-image takes shape based on input from other people, so distortion of that image can easily occur in instances where a group has little outside input. Assume a person demonstrates value through contrivance and can influence a faction of a cloistered group. An example might be a fraternity—a group that is as cloistered as it wants to be—in which one of the guys displays the trappings of wealth that everyone wants: Gucci wallet, Prada shirt, Rolex watch. Through this display, he then assumes *real* value to them. Perhaps they see the trappings as a sense of style, which could belong to either the natural or cultivated categories of demonstrated value. After awhile, they accept him as the leader, or at least endorse him. When his group accepts new members, or the group socializes with other

groups, he already has a power base. This power base provides real value, because he has the admiration of others. He does not have to use the contrivance that opened the door for him with the frat brothers. He now has concrete value as a stock to trade while humanizing himself. (Few people have the forethought to call out that the emperor's new clothes are phony.)

Think of Adolph Hitler. This is what he did in using the brownshirts to co-opt a nation. These paramilitary men played a major role in Hitler's rise to power after he successfully escalated their perception of his value. In effect, he leveraged a perceived value due to groupthink.

Simply having a good differentiator is not enough to create charisma. You need to know how to exploit the fact that you have a draw. Was the payroll soldier I described charismatic or just doing his job? Even though he had a ready-made fan club, he missed the boat when it came to charisma because he did not have a process map to follow, nor was he born with the instincts to create one.

Step 2: Recognize Opportunity

The finance clerk standing in front of the audience saw all of the people crowding him as nothing more than extra work. He projected onto many well-meaning people that they only wanted to talk to him because they needed information he had. The fact is that many may have just wanted to say "good job!" and give him an opportunity to practice this skill set. So the first lesson from Step 2 is this: Do not project. Open your eyes and look for chances to excel. In some cases opportunities are there, and you have blinded yourself to them. Imagine the outcome if Agent Piro had projected onto Saddam.

Your choice of target must reflect some knowledge that the person with whom you want to connect is predisposed to be receptive to your demonstration of value. There are many ways this can happen; the easiest is to recognize the body language that shows the person is interested in knowing more.

As a warm-up for the closer look at body language in Chapter 4, I want to give you the outline of gestures, posture, energy, and focus that convey inquisitiveness. With overt curiosity at one end and passing interest at the other, the state of inquisitiveness has a lot of degrees. As extreme as they may be, they still have some fundamental body language in common. What I describe here are the physical elements that a kid staring at a huge Christmas present has in common with an executive who receives an intra-office envelope marked "important."

⇨ Heightened energy.

⇨ Sharp focus on the object or person inciting inquisitiveness.

⇨ Raised eyebrows—even if that's just momentary— that signal surprise. This wouldn't apply, of course, if the executive with the "important" envelope got one of those twice a day when quarterly profits were announced.

⇨ Removal of barriers that may exist between the object of interest and the person. In the case of the child with the present, it would be moving things out of the way to get to the big gift, and then ripping through the wrapping paper. In the case of the person in the office, it would be placing the envelope in an accessible area on the desk and removing the contents from the envelope. When you're talking about gauging receptivity to you personally, the removal of a barrier could mean turning toward you, putting down or pushing aside an object that had come between you, uncrossing arms, or any other gesture that implies, "I trust you. We can be closer."

⇨ Reaching. This makes obvious sense if you're talking about a present or an envelope, but someone who simply wants to express inquisitiveness about you and your demonstrated value will instinctively want to "touch." Watch what your hands and head do at a museum, even when you know you cannot really come into contact with the Picasso. You reach—either with your hand or your whole body.

You can apply your skills of observation in concert with other ways to identify an opportunity, too. Use spotters; that is, people you know who are part of the same audience and tuned into your outcomes. They will often notice things you do not.

Look for examples of behavior other than inquisitiveness as you differentiate yourself. When someone walks up to you after a presentation and tells you what a fantastic job you have done, is that because she has a vested interest in your success, an infatuation with you as the "teacher," a curiosity about the subject matter, or wants to set you up for a critique that will slam you into self-esteem hell? Open your eyes, and turn off the projection that she is saying and doing what you want to see.

Step 3: Grant an Audience

You grant the person an audience, which could be a formal setup, such as a meeting; or an informal encounter, such as a conversation at the hors d'oeuvres table. Here is where you start to manage expectations, and your success in doing so rests in a paradox: Bring him close, but keep him at arm's length. This is the fan-dancing exercise. You want to show enough to demonstrate value, but not enough to lose your allure.

Your charisma depends on your target's perception of your value—something that sets you apart from the crowd. If you've developed a mnemonic for remembering all the presidents of the United States in chronological order, and then you divulge it to your target, the magic is gone. You suddenly become just another person because you gave away the special thing you had.

The real magic is already done for you. All that is left now is for you to not mess it up. If you managed to differentiate yourself by being smarter, faster, prettier, funnier, or more famous, all you have to do now is let the person know that you are just another person who is approachable, while still maintaining your value. This is easy enough for a Nobel Prize winner or former president, because their celebrity is a solid commodity. They can trade in that commodity while demonstrating their humanity. Unless you have an equally concrete superpower, your task is more difficult: to show the person you have value by subtly anchoring him to whatever it is that makes you worth bonding with. Keep in mind, however, that this may not be the same thing that allowed you to differentiate yourself in the beginning. The more layers you have to your personality, the more you have to work with. Lead with a good card, but keep the trump in reserve.

As the conversation flows, you act like the fan dancer, keeping the tantalizing secret in mind, but never fully disclosing it. One of the greatest differentiators and draws is *mystery*.

Balancing demonstrated value with humanity in order to create the peak opportunity in which a person feels comfortable approaching you is difficult when you have nothing of real value. It becomes much simpler when you have concrete value. A political leader might respond to your adulation with thanks for making him president. He walks a tightrope in terms of demonstrated value, because he concurrently reminds you that he is "divine," while he humanizes himself by showing a vulnerability; that is, that he needed *you* to get where he is. The balancing act not only ensures that you maintain the perception that there is a reason to admire you, but also to engender reasons not to fear you.

When these two are in balance, a person will feel invited to talk to you and even share information about herself.

Step 4: Create Belonging

Your target audience feels as though you are open to approach, and he sees you as human. Next, genuinely listen to what he has to say. If that seems simple, then you are likely a nimble conversationalist moving from one topic to the next. Get to understand who he is. Let him talk enough to find what you have in common and point it out. We all have something in common; if you listen long enough you can find it.

Maybe you know someone who lived four blocks away from his mother's cousin, or once dated a woman who went to school in a town nearby his hometown. Are those oblique facts the basis for a connection? Absolutely. If you are differentiated enough in the beginning, it is definitely enough. Remember that he is pursuing a normal course of connecting: finding common ground. He wants to bond with you because you have value; that is how you got to this step. You allow your target audience to create a belonging. He feels as though he matters to you, and as a result, draws closer to you and your "magic."

In the interrogation world, one of the key steps in achieving the desired outcome is establishing rapport; that is, coming to a common understanding. This definition deviates from the common social connotation, because rapport for interrogators means a conversational place with a framework that allows us to exchange ideas. There is no delusion of an oh-buddy-oh-pal relationship. One person is squarely in charge and the other understands the difference in status.

Nevertheless, the bond between interrogator and source can occur very quickly. It centers on the source's understanding that the interrogator accepts her on some level, no matter how superficial. If language abilities, knowledge of the source's operations, and other "magic" seem to place the interrogator so far above her as to make the interrogator seem unreachable, she needs to remind the source of common ground. This does not mean accepting her as an equal in the magic. The interrogator simply finds territory where the two can relate authentically. He builds a framework that enables sharing ideas. Rapport is a bridge.

Do not continue to bond and build rapport indefinitely or, similar to the interrogator that tells all up front, you lose your magic. Get your target to the point where she feels comfortable with telling you why she is different and important. You will recognize it when the opportunity arises. When you let her talk about him, you appear magnanimous. This is not difficult, and I will even give you tools for active listening in Chapter 4 in the event your first tries do not yield what you think they should.

Step 5: Differentiate Your Target

When he feels comfortable enough to talk to you, it means you have enough rapport for him to have a sense of belonging. He has established himself in terms of you and him, and he is ready to build on that.

Humans bleed information when we talk. One of the toughest things to teach a young interrogator is how to hide what he is looking for. Preoccupation with our own thoughts causes us to drop key words and concepts as we talk about other things. So even when asking questions, we often telegraph information that's running though our minds. In the interrogation business, we call this leakage "source leads."

You have a natural skill set to follow up on these, and this book gives you the techniques to refine it. When you are in a conversation at a party, do you notice how a good conversation flows like a stream, following the contours of the land on either side? That is an example of how following up on a source lead works: Watch where he goes with his expressed thoughts. When he telegraphs that something is important, prod him to elaborate. By allowing your target to express his ideas and opinions and differentiate himself, you can teleport him from one level to another on Maslow's Hierarchy. The resultant feeling you generate will cause him to feel as though you have some kind of magic, or to paraphrase Arthur C. Clarke, your technique is sufficiently advanced.

It's difficult to pull off the demonstration of value consistently if you're in the public eye, and by that I don't mean someone as famous as Brad Pitt, who has people around him reinforcing his public image as a super-sexy, super-talented, and super-philanthropic man. I mean someone in a company who has the daily scrutiny of bosses, colleagues, and employees. Their input on a daily basis can hammer your presentation of value.

So, if you want to sustain this, you need to manage and insulate the egos of people around you; that is, to get them to focus on your value as a kind of gold standard—the criterion against which others are measured. This sounds hard, but if you look around at the people who accomplish this on a daily basis, you will realize that it can be very easy. If you went into the tiger cage every day, then that's the standard of differentiation. If you had the most intriguing photos in your PowerPoint presentations every week, then that would be the standard. Do you recognize this technique? You are creating a snowball effect that will allow others to see you as valuable, and give you tangible stock to trade.

EXERCISE: DEBUNK THE VALUE

Give yourself distance from demonstration of value and note the effect that it has on your relationship with the person. If you can short-circuit the "value step" in someone you meet, notice the reduction of their charismatic effect on you. Now that you know the steps to charisma, you can use that to control your responses. Realize that the more concrete the differentiator, the harder it will be to resist. I know people who hated Bill Clinton for his policies, but upon meeting him, each was enamored.

In summary, charisma is not some magical aura residing in the person at all. It is an ability to move others up the Hierarchy of Needs, quickly manipulating them to go from belonging to status. Ultimately, charisma is an effect living in the subject. After all, as you leave them with the feeling of having known the x-iest (brightest, sexiest, wittiest) person alive, you have given them some value, and they can become more charismatic.

Most people are not exercising skills so they intentionally appear charismatic. I think that most people stumbled into a set of processes that gives them the capability to accomplish the outcome that you recognize as charisma. I do not think this is the manifestation of some sinister personality streak, but rather an intelligent polishing of a process that occurs through time.

This mechanical cycle, similar to any other process, will require that you refine it. You cannot expect that you will go from ordinary and bland on Day One to Bill Clinton next week. You need to work through the steps you need to inventory, whether you have natural, cultivated, or contrived value. And if you have natural value it never hurts to add a layer of cultivated value, because people will respect it even more. If all you have now is contrived value, take time to cultivate value as you follow this process.

Charisma From a Distance

Given that there is a formula for charisma that follows the steps I've outlined, how can a person have charisma from a distance? You probably never met John F. Kennedy or Princess Diana when they were alive, nor have you chatted with Barack Obama, Bill Clinton, or Queen Elizabeth II. The formula is still the same. The difference is that these people have the international spotlight, and you are falling for the message delivered by the image, which, interestingly enough, is no different from what you would get if you did meet them in person. Most of us will never know the real person, simply the aspect of that complex person that he wants us to see. They are still showing you their value, granting you an audience via the media, and making you feel as though you belong. In the case of a politician, he allows you the chance to differentiate by associating yourself with someone grand or a cause so grand. The more inflated this feeling, the more you will be willing to invest your time and money in his success.

The Opposite of Charisma

The opposite of charisma is behavioral bad breath—a lazy, obnoxious state that repels, but does not give a forceful shove. Similar to charisma, you might describe it as "very difficult to define accurately," or an "elusive, even indefinable, personality trait." The difference is that trait arouses a sense of distance, not the perception of intimacy. Whatever it is, this is not a characteristic you want to try to achieve, even if you want to get rid of someone. Hence, there is no section here on "the mechanics of the opposite of charisma." Although, there are plenty of instances in which a celebrity seems to operate with anti-charisma. People are drawn to that celebrity simply because he's famous and/or talented, but he never humanizes himself, and instead rebuffs his fans. Hollywood is strewn with the ghosts of celebrities who made the ultimate mistake of turning on their admirers before having enough clout to casually blow off the little people.

In moving someone out of your life, you will learn to use the mechanics of charisma to move someone down the Hierarchy of Needs if you want to take a negative approach, or maneuver him up into another peer group if you want to take a positive approach.

SECTION II

Tools of the Trade

CHAPTER 4

Tools to Get What You Want

Interrogators get a sophisticated set of tools to use when questioning prisoners. When I am asked what interrogation is, I often describe it as nothing more than extreme interpersonal skills. This set of tools is finite, and the process of putting them to work, describable. I want to stress that your use of them will not catch most people off-guard—it will go unnoticed because most people have no knowledge of them.

All of these tools come from the world of interrogation, where we learned them as effective ways to influence human behavior. Interrogators get little more than what is covered in this chapter; you are getting a comprehensive look at using them to make people do what you *want*.

By starting out with a focus on human drives—that is, why the approach detailed in this book works—I set the stage for some very complex lessons that I have learned from years of interrogating and teaching people to resist interrogation. Most interrogators do not do both; they are not exposed to psychologists or given the opportunity to teach resistance skills. As a result, most interrogators never get the benefit of these lessons. They do not get the kind of in-depth look at why things work in concert with a high-level look at the primary tools of interrogation. Think of this chapter as a primer on the tools, with the specifics on applying them in later chapters.

If you want more detail about the tools themselves and illustrations of how you can apply them in a variety of personal and professional relationships, then you need to invest in the original books (written by us) *How to Spot a Liar* and *I Can Read You Like a Book*. They are aimed at helping you boost your abilities as a negotiator, sales pro, seducer, politician, lawyer, or parent.

In this condensed presentation, I will take a systematic approach to learning the tools with the specific aim of getting people to do what you want. Starting with basic and working to complex, I will show you how they fit together to effect influence quickly.

The tools you need fall into five categories:

1. Questioning.
2. Psychological levers or approaches
3. Body language/baselining.
4. Probing.
5. Active listening.

Interrogators use all of these to extract information and influence behavior by managing a person's emotional state. Learning to question effectively not only allows an interrogator to extract factual information, but also to establish the framework of context in which the source understands the information. Questioning also allows the interrogator to maneuver the source into position to apply an approach, that is, a psychological lever or style of manipulation that changes depending on what you know about the person's needs, desires, personality, and mental state. Once an interrogator understands the source and the source is cooperating, the interrogator can use the combination of approach and masterful questioning to pare down the source's options and gain compliance. A command of body language both gives the interrogator insights into the unspoken communication of a source and allows him to realign the dynamic with the source. A keen understanding of nonverbal messaging allows the interrogator to know when the source is buying the approach and when to back off. Through orchestrated use of these extreme interpersonal skills, an interrogator transforms an enemy into a reliable source of information.

Questioning

You might think of questions like a leash on a dog. In some cases, the leash gently links a man and a dog; the leash suggests to the dog where to go. In others, it gives the man a way to pull the dog in the direction he wants. And in others, the man who doesn't know what he's doing gets pulled along by the dog.

I sort questions like this: direct, control, repeat, leading, compound, canned, negative, and vague. Interrogators are taught to never use some of these, but at some point, all of them will be useful to you.

Good questions are easy to understand and use basic interrogatives: who, what, when, where, why, how, what else, and when all else fails, "huh?" Good questions allow the person to answer in a narrative, so you can gather information. When your purpose is to corral a conversation, a leading, vague, or compound question may be of more use. Questions can be used as steering mechanisms to direct your target to a point where you can apply a psychological approach.

Direct Questions

Just ask what you want to know—a good question allows the person to answer in a narrative format. Most questions you ask will be this type. The longer the answer, the more options you have to pick up your next question from the information deposited in the answer. That is, you follow the lead.

Control Questions

Control questions are questions to which you know the answer. In the intelligence business, we use these to establish whether or not the person is telling the truth. I simply ask, "Where were you on Tuesday?" to see if the source will lie to me, or to see what his body language looks like when he responds truthfully. The use of control questions is limitless.

A good interrogator uses them to redirect conversation or to apply pressure to the source to create stress and verify veracity.

Repeat Questions

Simply restating or stating the same question in another way is a repeat question. Repeat questions are another way to verify whether the source is lying. If he gives you different answers each time, he is lying. A sophisticated version of this tool slices the question into pieces, which gets at different nuances of the answer, and then consolidates the multiple answers to get the whole picture.

Leading Questions

Interrogators are taught to avoid these questions as a matter of practice, because leading questions telegraph what you want to hear. Ironically, to be any good at getting people to give you information, you need them to talk first—leading questions can serve that purpose. Maneuvering someone into a position that allows you to successfully use a psychological lever often requires luring someone down a conversational path. Leading questions are most beneficial in setting up the follow-up question; they result in a yes or no answer. Many involve the verb "to be," as in this leading question posed by Dan Rather to Saddam Hussein: "Mr. President, do you expect to be attacked by an American-led invasion?" (CBS, February 24, 2003). Unless you are deliberately trying to lead your target, beginning a question with something such as "will you," "did you," or "are you" indicates you need to restructure your question. Leading questions have value in establishing control in a conversation because they are structured to help you slip past a logic point that someone might have an issue with.

Compound Questions

This is another question style interrogators are taught to stay away from because it is confusing. For instance, "Did you go to the store or the bank?" When you ask this, he should answer with one or the other; however, if he is uncertain of what you are asking, he can escape by saying no. Remember the science of interrogation is about getting the most information in the least amount of time. For our purposes, the compound question can be part of the *art* of interrogation

You can really throw a person off balance with a compound question. You could ask an employee, for example, "Did you make those cold calls or finish the paperwork on the Smith contract?" That leaves him trying to second-guess you about which action you consider more important. It could be the first step in getting him to stay late to do whichever thing he hasn't done yet as he tries to interpret your meaning.

Canned Questions

I would call this more a style of preparation than specific brand of question. Interrogators are often asked to become an expert on a subject in a couple of hours. As a result, interrogators prepare questions ahead of time to give them the right vernacular and the right context. In your world, canned questions can be useful, especially when confronting a person with his own words or navigating a complex social issue.

Negative Questions

Do you not like Hillary Clinton?

How does a person answer a question like this? Does the answer carry any real meaning to anyone other than the asker? This is another type of question that interrogators are taught to stay away from because it creates confusion. When you are trying to manipulate someone, however, confusion may be just what you are after. Keep this one in your tool kit.

Vague Questions

In the interrogation environment, any question not containing precise names, dates, and circumstances can be considered a vague question. For example, "Were you with them?" In terms of plain language, conversation questions such as this are the norm, and they work fine because everyone understands the context. No one is trying to gain the upper hand by being misleading or evasive. In manipulation or interrogation, however, both agendas may be present. Intentionally or unintentionally, the use of ambiguous pronouns or concepts can lead to a misunderstanding on the part of either party. The person wielding the question, who wants to throw someone off track, might jump into the middle of a conversation about expense accounts and new people in the sales department with: "Do you take advantage of them?" The receiver might trap himself in front of his boss with a response such as, "I travel so much for this company that I probably have from time to time." When the questioner replies, "Oh, really? I was making a joke about the new hires," then no one at the table knows whether the question was ill-phrased and innocent, or subterfuge.

EXERCISE: HOW THE PROS DO IT

Listen to snippets of interviews on Larry King Live *or late-night comedy shows, and flag the types of questions asked. Categorize the questions, not only for type, but also on the basis of whether the "bad" questions were artfully used.*

Aside from extracting information about issues, questions can give you insights into the individual. They are also powerful tools for managing conversation. In moving a conversation toward the outcome of uncovering facets of an individual, you can use a range of questioning styles that people in a negotiation, for example, should *not* use. When you think someone is being deceptive, or you need just bare facts, take the interrogators' path and avoid the questions they avoid—leading, compound, and negative. Interrogators and people who need to keep information pure often sound like machines as they go about extracting information in daily life.

Also consider your audience. Is the person you are about to question a clock-driven efficiency expert? Or a big-picture, artsy type for whom details do not matter? Or is she so detail-oriented that clocks and the big picture are immaterial? The questions not only have to make sense to you, but also to your target if you want a clean and simple answer. You need to ask in a way that she can access the information in the way it was stored and, therefore, respond easily. When you are after information, you should create questions and flow to take into account how your target thinks, but when you want to take her off balance or confuse her, you should alter the style to force her out of her comfort zone.

Questioning Strategy

Understanding how each of the question types fit into an overall plan makes each question you ask a building block for the next.

1. Think before you open your mouth, no matter what style of questioning you are using at the moment. If you have a lot of questions you need to ask, but your brain hasn't prepared them properly, your strategy will fail you; you will not have good flow that your target can follow and, more importantly, you will end up chasing butterflies.

2. You can deliberately use a splatter pattern and ask questions that seem to go all over, but ultimately elicit the information you need. That's ideal if you are concerned that you will not get

straight answers from linear, well-directed questioning that shows your intent.

3. Ask the "next question." Don't ask, "Are you married?" Ask, "What's your wife's name?" Use common sense, though. You can look like a fool if you ask the wrong next step.

EXERCISE: WHY THE PROS DO IT

Tune in again to Larry King Live *or one of the other big interview shows. This time take a big-picture look. Follow his questions and see if you can find the magic behind what he is doing. Can you see his intent from the questions he is asking? Is there a master plan hidden behind that rambling, or is he just asking disconnected questions that enquiring minds want to know? If you can spot the agenda, keep that in the back of your head as you go about designing your questioning strategy. Others may be looking for your agenda, too.*

Questions are tools for driving conversation. As you go about planning your strategy to deal with someone, these tools will become invaluable. As you go about your day, ask yourself how effectively you are questioning. Are the interrogatives your guides, or do you follow every butterfly you see, wondering "why?" at every juncture just like a three year old?

"Why?" is a good question that is often answered by other interrogatives. Using the word *why* rarely gets the same defining answer as discerning the why. If I ask you the when, what, how, and who questions first, you will get the why.

⇨   Who was John Brown?

⇨   When did he live?

⇨   What did he do?

⇨   How was he killed?

⇨   Who was killed with him?

Someone who answers these questions will eventually give you the answer to "why was John Brown killed?"

Psychological Levers or Approaches

Although the U.S. Army refers to them as approaches, I want you to think of these techniques as ways to pry your way into the psyche of a person, and that's why the term "levers" helps anchor the concept. With some basic understanding of any person, you can choose one or more of these approaches to get a desired effect from your target.

The styles of exercising psychological leverage over someone might be grouped into two categories: intimidating and persuading. The Army lists at least 14 different interrogation approaches, but the ones that have relevance to "normal" personal and professional interactions are the following 10 approaches.

Intimidating

1. **Direct.** You ask straight questions about what you want to know. This is really not so much of an approach as a demand in interrogation terms. It says, "You know who I am and here is what I want." The same may hold true for you remembering that, just like an aboveboard leader, you may ask for incremental changes without divulging your long-term objective.

2. **Fear-up.** In this context, I will focus only on the level that interrogators call "fear-up mild," because its companion, "fear-up harsh," is never appropriate in daily life. A human resources manager may use fear-up mild with an employee caught in an indiscretion: "Will you come clean with me about this, or would you rather discuss it with my boss, who has the authority to fire you on the spot?"

3. **Silence.** Imagine a stage onto which your subject has just been dropped; all eyes are on her, and she has no idea what her line is. This is the kind of feeling you can create by simply asking a tough question and providing no assistance in getting an answer.

Persuading

4. **Fear-down.** You rush to stop someone's emotional bleeding. You might think, "Well that's nice. How

could that be construed as psychological manipulation?" It is if you do it with the intent of gaining the person's trust so that you can influence his behavior. This is often used in conjunction with fear-up mild to create a sort of good cop/bad cop approach.

5. **Incentive.** Offer the person something he really, really wants, such as an invitation to play golf in your foursome that includes the company CEO. In interrogations, it may be nothing more than milk and cookies. In non-interrogation environments, the more differentiating, the better.

6. **Emotional.** Use strong emotions against the person; for example, if she loves her job more than anything else in the world then convince her that doing something your way will make her the company hero. The emotional key can also involve the opposite; that is, hatred of something or someone. Play heavily on belonging and differentiation with this one. If she loves something, she will want to nurture and hold onto it; if she hates something, she will want to distance herself from it.

7. **Pride-and-ego (up-or-down).** You either inflate or deflate a person's ego with this style. We all know the power of a compliment, but the putdown can also be effective with the right person. You don't want to use the negative approach with an insecure, inept person to get him on your side.

He probably already knows that he's working with deficits, so all you will do is alienate him. The intent is that when you make someone feel special, he wants to earn the compliment. When you make someone feel inadequate, he wants to prove you wrong. Mastery of these two approaches is key to fracturing and bonding.

8. **We-know-all.** When you do the *right* homework before meeting with a person, you can seem to know much more than you do. For example, with tools such as Google Earth, you know details about someone's neighborhood. That kind of knowledge can position you as either someone with whom they can bond, because you're on top of things, or someone to fear.

9. **Futility.** Preying on a person's doubts, cultivating more doubts, and then moving in for the "kill" are the hallmarks of this approach. In daily life, this one preys well on the fact that, while we love underdogs, no one likes to be on the losing team.

10. **Repetition.** You ask the same thing over and over. You can do it by repeating the same question exactly, or by introducing new words that circle around the same idea. One question that lends itself to this kind of psychological bruising is, "What do you think we can do to improve sales?" In a business or personal setting, this repetition likely occurs through time, not in the form of back-to-back questions to a mind-numbingly, incessant beat as it would be done in an interrogation.

Each of these levers, or combination of these levers, is a valuable tool when targeted to the individual. What you need to do for now is understand the concepts of the tools, so that we have common language to use in the application of levers to individuals. By using the right questions you can set up opportunities to apply each of these levers to get the opening you want. So how do you know it is working? I find that by looking at the person to whom I am talking and noticing changes in response, both intentional and unintentional, I can understand just how far to push or when to back off.

Body Language/Baselining

A fundamental skill you will need to use all of the tools in this book effectively is baselining. I define baselining as determining how a person behaves and speaks under normal circumstances. Only when you understand what is normal for your target can you spot a change.

So what's normal? In a situation with little or no stress present, people will use the vocal tone and cadence, word choices, and movements that are normal *for them*. That doesn't mean what *you* consider normal, or what *you* think should be normal, but what is normal *for them*. I can say things such as, "That's the worst example of butt snorkeling I've seen this year," and people in a meeting won't think that's odd. They think, "That's Hartley." If Maryann said that, people would think she was (a) drunk, (b) imitating me, or (c) extremely nervous. Step one in baselining, therefore, is to engage a person in an environment, and a topic, that keeps the exchange relaxed, or at least makes few demands emotionally and intellectually. Use nonthreatening questions that start a conversation on a relaxed note.

When you baseline, it's a deliberate action. You set up a situation in which you converse and move with intent. As a result, you gain significant knowledge about a person's behavior, speech patterns, body language, and energy level. This baseline gives you a template for using the other tools in the interrogator's tool box. When you see change, you know the other tools are working. I deliberately present this material to you in this fashion because few interrogators have the skills to baseline and read body language, but yet they are successful using only questioning and approaches. By learning to baseline you add to your skill set and compound the effectiveness of the other tools.

Voice

To baseline the voice, listen for tone, pitch, cadence, word choice, and use of fillers sounds such as "um" and "ah," or filler words such as *like*, *basically*, or any other meaningless place holder.

⇨   **Tone.** If your mother said, "Please go outside" to you as a child, her tone of voice told you everything you needed to know. With a calm, quiet demeanor, it could be an invitation to see a new puppy. But with a clipped, harsh tone, it could suggest a strong, sarcastic warning not to touch the door handle. Tone is about lilt of voice and stress on words. Tone indicates the meaning of words, regardless of which words were spoken. If you have a pet, try telling your pet in happy tones, "I am so mad at you, I'm going to give you away to a stranger." What's his response? The tone makes it all sound like, "I love you, Fluffy." We have all heard this admonition from a parent or partner: it is not what you said, it is how you said it.

EXERCISE: JUST LISTEN

Turn off your eyes for the moment. Do not try to predict what your target's body language means. You want to do this so you get audio only and eliminate the distraction of the person to whom you're listening.

Tune into interviews on NPR such as "Terry Gross's Fresh Air." Listen to a couple of celebrities talk during interviews that seem low-key and friendly. Character- ize their vocal patterns in that relatively relaxed state. Contrast that pattern with the sound of their voice when they are agitated or acting agitated. Note the effect that stress has on the voice.

➡ **Cadence.** The rate at which someone speaks cor-relates to what's going on in his head. Determine his normal pace and listen for change. A New Jersey native in Georgia stands out, as does a Georgia native in New Jersey. Once you estab-lish the norm for him, deviations indicate some-thing has changed in his head.

➡ **Pitch.** Agitation, passion for a topic, and uncer-tainty all cause the pitch to rise. Again, this is a common response to such emotions, but the im-portant point is that you become aware of the shift. John Lovitz practically founded a career on this pitch swing in the 1980s as *Saturday Night Live*'s "lying guy."

➡ **Word choice.** Look for changes in pattern. Most people (especially those without writers) consis-tently use the same words or word styles. Few people dramatically alter word patterns without a change in the thought process. Using simple words is typically a choice for clear communica-tion, so when you see the pattern shift to a few Oxford nuggets in an unnatural way, or move quickly from speech reflecting a rich vocabulary to "shucks" and "golly," these are indicators of stress. As baseball star Roger Clemens sat be-fore Congress testifying about steroid use, you could hear him trying to navigate the minefield of liability as he answered representatives' ques-tions. The result was a mangled English response

with tense pronoun shift and a barely compre-
hensible message. All are signs of high stress.

Some of the other vocal cues you should heed in baselining involve enunciation, elaboration, and trailing.

If you remember how your mom enunciated every word when she chastised you for not doing your homework, you have an idea of how stress can affect that vocal pattern. The opposite can be true, too, so you find a person deviating from his baseline by mumbling. Enunciation can also relate to accents. President Bush's speech is always accented, with the pronunciations of words dripping with Texas twang. It's that way whether or not he seems stressed, which is not the case for some people, who will either revert to a heavier accent or move away from it when they feel stressed. Regarding elaboration, ask yourself why a person who typically rambles on with details would suddenly give clipped responses? Or why would a person who seems to use words surgically suddenly turn into a rambler? Finally, some people trail their sentences as a matter of course, but others only do it when they don't want you to hear what they're saying. Whatever the cause, something's different from the baseline.

Eyes Are Windows to the Soul

If words and speech patterns can suggest what someone is thinking, then eyes can tell you where they are going inside their heads to retrieve the words.

Baselining movement means paying attention to gestures and twitches from head to toe, but it also involves taking note of where the eyes go in response to certain kinds of questions. When humans think, our eyes move around the head. Most Americans think breaking eye contact is a sign of deception, but, in effect, it is a sign that you have asked a good question that requires thought. In other words, eye movement signals that someone is accessing a particular portion of her brain. With a few easy steps you can discern which portion.

My hypothesis is that the structure of the brain may be an indicator as to why these patterns of eye movement occur. The visual cortex is toward the back of the head, so typically people will look up high past the brow ridge and to one side or the other when accessing visual cues. The processors for sound are over the ears, so most people will look only slightly up and to one side for auditory cues. Emotion and calculation are special cases that I'll examine after the basic discussion.

Questioning to Baseline Eye Movement

I want you to pay attention to your own eyes as you answer this next question: What were the last words you heard on the phone?

As you answer, you will likely find your eyes drifting slightly up and to your left. If you deviated from that it was likely slightly up and to the right, or down and to the right if the words you heard were charged with emotion. I know that because roughly 90 percent of people react one way—looking to the left—and 10 percent the other. That is unless it is an emotional issue.

I used a question that forced you to recall something, rather than make something up. Because I cannot see your eyes, and you have no reason to lie to yourself, the question was an easy one requiring a simple fact. But what if you ask a person that question and a true response would be embarrassing or incriminating? She might make up something, and the eye movement response would be different.

In determining what a person's eye movement pattern for truth is versus the pattern for imagination, you would baseline by starting with a question to which you know the answer. For example, what is the fifth word of the "The Star Spangled Banner."

The four steps to the baselining process are simple:

1. **Ask good, solid control questions that elicit a narrative memory response.** This means you should ask the person a question to which you know the answer. Ask a question that will require some thought, though, not something that's such common knowledge (because no thought will go into the answer).

2. **Ask questions that isolate a single sense.** Because the brain isolates processors for the senses, you can ask questions that cause the person to access each individual sense memory independent of the other. Questions about lyrics to songs make a good basis for exercising auditory recall. Things such as driving directions to a landmark or descriptions of people you both know are good

visual questions. This need not be contrived. Say something such as, "A person I work with asked me how I would describe Bob physically [note: you need to pick an ordinary looking person for this], and I had a hard time with it. What would you say?" This gives a challenge, and allows the person to show you their capabilities.

3. **Steer away from emotional issues when baselining visual and auditory.** Stay away from questions that evoke anger, passion, or a recollection of trauma. For instance, if you ask about a recently deceased parent of a divorced spouse you will likely get mixed signals.

4. **Observe and make note of where his eyes go to access memory.** Once you get baseline auditory memory and visual memory, you will find the creative side, where imagination flavors the output, in the same place, but the opposite direction.

My observations through the years have convinced me that most people will look to their left for memory and to their right for construct. That means with good, solid control questions such as, "What is the fifth word of the national anthem?" most people will look slightly up (between cheek and brow) and to their left. Once you get this, you know the auditory construct accessing cue will be slightly up and to the right. If they access auditory memory on the left, they will also access visual memory on the left. The reliability of your results relies solely on using good questioning, and then mapping responses. Memory right, or memory left—that's all it is.

EXERCISE: WATCH THE EYES

Practice the technique of baselining eye movement with friends and strangers. Casually insert the kinds of questions that stimulate visual and auditory recall, as well as visual and auditory creativity.

Here are some sample questions to get you started:

1. *What does your bathroom wallpaper look like? (visual memory)*
2. *What is the 10th word of "The Star Spangled Banner"? (auditory memory)*
3. *What do you think the surface of Saturn looks like? (visual construct)*
4. *What sound does a giraffe make when it's mating? (auditory construct)*

The two special accessing cues are emotion and calculation. I have never seen deviation in these. Emotion is down and to the person's right. Calculation is down and to the person's left.

You can use this knowledge of which part of the brain a person uses to create a baseline. Knowing this will give you a decided edge in using the tools of interrogation, because you'll be able to spot "creative" answers to questions that should be factual. Just having that information, and not necessarily even calling someone on it, gives you the upper hand in any kind of exchange.

Observe what other facial signs are normal for your subject. I know someone who has a periodic eye twitch associated with nerve damage. That's normal for him, rather than a sign of stress. How a person smiles is part of the baseline, too. My normal smile is a kind of crooked half-smile, but when I'm on television or making a presentation, I'll deliberately use a more even smile because people commonly interpret that as a trustworthy expression.

The Body Speaks the Mind's Thoughts

Read body language to measure how successful you have been using the psychological keys and questioning. Use body language to amplify your success. This section focuses on the former to prepare you for applying your knowledge of body language in a proactive way.

By offering you snapshots of key body language from forehead to toe, you will get a sense of the pieces and parts that make up expressions of suspicion, resistance, acceptance, and other emotions relevant to getting people to do what you want. You need to know, for example, when someone is subconsciously signaling that what you are doing has caused her pain; you will have to back off before you can regain leverage with her. Critical factors that shape expressions of emotion are energy and focus.

Reading body language accurately means that you have to know how and when to pull yourself out of the equation. Reading someone else's body language involves a paradox when you are interacting with someone: It's all about you and never about you. It's all about you in the sense that you provoked a response, and need to understand that response in order to continue the process of bonding or fracturing. It's never about you in the sense that you cannot project what a person's gestures, posture, and vocal characteristics mean based on how you express certain emotions. Remember to baseline. You always have to keep in mind the unique ways other people, and you, use the body to communicate. Sometimes a scratch just means there's an itch; other times, you're the figurative itch.

The exception is certain involuntary and universal movements, which convey consistent messages. One that you probably see every day is the eyebrow flash signaling, "I know you!" or, "I've heard that before." I have seen prisoners who denied knowing each other do this quick raise of the brows upon seeing each other unexpectedly, and it became such a reliable and consistent piece of body language that I codified the meaning as a sign of recognition. I have also seen this on the street, in stores, and in meetings. Knowledge of this momentary raising of the eyebrows gives you a distinct advantage in assessing which people and ideas someone instantly bonds with.

The Big Four

Your starting point is the four basic categories of moves: illustrators, regulators, adaptors, and barriers.

Illustrators

Body language helps your mouth say what you mean. From punching the air when your team scores a touchdown to showing with your hand and arm how steps wind around in a circular staircase, there are innumerable ways you use illustrators.

Maryann spent Super Bowl XLII with a born-and-bred New Yorker whose arms, legs, and voice illustrated exactly how he felt about the Giants's performance. As you go through the other categories of gestures in this section, keep in mind that he didn't show any of them except illustrators: every move spotlighted an emotion. Illustrators are the mind punctuating thought; in fact, think of them as servants of the mind. Look for these to support the words a person is saying. When the two begin to diverge, you have an issue.

This is a great opportunity to appreciate cultural differences, by the way. For example, men with a Germanic background tend to use illustrators that are close to the body, with arms that stay below the shoulders (typical of what you see in the mid-Western United States). But men of Mediterranean or Hispanic heritage will comfortably gesture with the arms higher.

EXERCISE: ILLUSTRATE YOUR FEELINGS

Ask someone you trust to observe you in conversation. Give that person permission to do it without warning, and then listen to what that person says about the way you move when you are making a point. If you get to a point where they notice a deviation in the way your words and physical punctuation mesh, think back to what caused it. Was your mind in one place and your mouth in another?

Regulators

You can overtly regulate conversation, as many moms do, by putting a finger to your lips, doing a zip-the-lips motion, or moving your arm in a big circle to indicate "speed it up." You may also use regulators more subtly by pursing your lips when you would like someone to stop talking, or nodding vigorously as a way of encouraging the person's words to come out faster.

EXERCISE: STOPPER IN A DRAIN

Watch what people do in a meeting when someone bores them with a retread, whether it's a whole presentation that almost everyone has heard before, or a just a piece of one. Some regulators will leak out because people simply cannot help themselves: the pen tapping on the table, the finger pressed hard against the lips. Others will be quite deliberate: interruption with a question that goes off-topic, the boss moving his hand across his throat to signal "cut."

Adaptors

Adaptors are ways to release nervous energy, and too numerous to list even in an encyclopedia of body language. Many of the ways people use the body to ease discomfort are idiosyncratic, but common adaptors include vigorous rubbing moves by men—hands, arms, legs, neck; and petting moves by women—a softer version of the rubbing gestures that men use. Other adaptors can be picking at cuticles, foot tapping, and nervous shuffling. When you see moves such as these, you know that the person is unconsciously taking action to adapt to his environment. As you learn more about using body language, you'll know whether seeing adaptors means you are getting the reaction you want, or pushing the wrong buttons.

EXERCISE: SIT STILL FOR A CHANGE

Most people have limited awareness of the idiosyn-cratic things they do to ease discomfort in a new situa-tion. The next time you are in a meeting or at a social gathering with new people, pay attention to what your body wants to do—rubbing, shuffling, moving of pen-cils or forks, or whatever your impulse is at the mo-ment. This time, just don't do it. Do you find the impulse leaking out in another way such as some kind of fidget-ing, or are you sitting there, perfectly still, thinking that you might explode?

Barriers

The requirement for personal space depends on circum-stances, as well as the people around you. In some cases, space is not enough; you need a barrier. Putting an arm, computer bag, newspaper, desk, or anything else between you and an-other person constitutes a barrier. A barrier is never a sign of acceptance, although when your target puts up a barrier, that's not necessarily a bad thing. You have created an opportunity. It could mean that you hit a sore spot and, once you back off and see the barrier go down, you can effectively use a pressure-release tactic to get what you want. This is similar to the good cop/bad cop approach.

EXERCISE: MY BEER GLASS, MY FRIEND

Go to a public place where you can watch sponta-
neous social interaction, such as a party or a bar. Watch
how people guard their space even though they are in-
volved in intense conversations, as well as how some
people lay down the barriers and invite people in—even
strangers. Are you starting to see how some people
express the desire for connection cautiously, whereas
others could not be more obvious?

Face and Mood

You can broadcast disbelief, confusion, surprise, anger, and a host of other emotions just by moving your eyebrows— unless you've had Botox injections. As I go through brief de- scriptions of the movements, look in the mirror and see the range of states you can capture by moving nothing more than your brows.

⇨ **Wrinkled brow**—People commonly wrinkle their brow in thought. Add a little eye movement, and different emotions surface. A wrinkled brow with eyes sharply focused on a person looks more like outrage or utter disbelief. A wrinkled brow with eyes to the side is one way of saying, "You can't mean that."

➡ **Knit brow**—Anger, concern, and fear are just three of the emotions that come through with a knit brow. Again, a slight shift in where the eyes are focused, along with a tilt of the head, can make all the difference. Here's another factor to add that interrogators see a lot: If the person has enough emotion to be in fight-or-flight mode, the pupils will dilate to take in more information about the imminent threat or target. This is an involuntary response that animals have to the approach of a predator. Combine a wrinkled or knit brow with a drawn mouth, or the corners of the mouth pulled downward, and you have drawn some serious disbelief or even disgust.

➡ **Arched eyebrow**—From *Star Trek*'s Mr. Spock to your second-grade teacher, people can project very different meanings with an arched eyebrow. Spock frequently accompanied his look with the word *interesting*. It's more likely your second-grade teacher did it in combination with a jaundiced eye and slight smirk to indicate that she really did not believe your hamster ate your homework.

➡ **Two arched eyebrows**—Here's a gesture you have seen thousands of times on every kind of person, from the new hire giving a presentation to the president of the United States giving the State of the Union address. This lifting and holding of both eyebrows is another one of those involuntary and universal pieces of body language that I've observed: the request for approval. This is an eyebrow raise that signals uncertainty. It is often accompanied by an auditory clue as well: The person makes a statement that sounds a lot like a question. Whether or not they actually ask, "You believe me, right?," that is the implication. The important thing to note about the request for approval is that the person is asking how *you* perceive what he is saying. The raising of the eyebrows with a slight pause that captures the look of request-for-approval is an eternity in terms of facial expressions, which are generally fleeting.

That brings me to a few that are the opposite of request-for-approval—both involuntary and universal. These are examples of deliberate and/or culturally specific types of facial body language that involve the mouth:

⇨ **Smile**—A genuine smile engages the muscles of the temple. As people age, it's easy to tell how much authentic expression of joy they've experienced, unless they've had the help of plastic surgery or some excellent eye cream. In contrast, a "professional" smile involves only the lower part of the face; it looks insincere. The person has a grin, but conveys no happiness. In the United

States, a smile is a tool to project openness, pleas-
antness, sexiness, and a lot of other "-nesses." In
other words, it's expected on certain occasions;
the smile is a planned and calculated event. When
you see *that* smile, you know it is not part of the
body language of acceptance. Be cautious: the
person may still be trying to figure out whether
or not you're okay, there may be real disdain for
you, or perhaps she thinks she can manipulate
you by appearing to be friendly. Chimps smile
out of fear—and we are related to them.

EXERCISE: SMILE FOR THE CAMERA

*This is a two-part exercise. First, go to a newsstand
and look at the covers of magazines, especially the ones
inhabited by celebrities. How many of them have a smile
that engages the temples, that is, a smile that puts lines
around the eyes? What feeling do you get from seeing
those few who do versus those who smile for the camera, but not the public?*

*For the second part of the exercise, watch some in-
terview shows on TV or the Internet. Pay attention to
how a celebrity warms up to the interview and goes from
a professional smile to a genuine smile. That's the magic
of a good interviewer—to be able to arouse the humanity of the famous person so you feel the authenticity. What
happens if your celebrity never gets to that point?*

➡ **Smirk**—A closed mouth drawn straight to the side or down at the corner conveys disgust, particularly when combined with a wrinkled brow. In concert with an arched brow, as I said previously in relation to the schoolteacher, you have a credibility problem. Mix it up with eyes tightly closed and you see a look of pain. In short, a smirk is a deliberate centerpiece of a number of emotional expressions. What do these all have in common, though? They are negative. The closed mouth serves as a barrier, while the rest of the face explains something about the barrier that is there.

➡ **Lips parted**—Fashion magazines have pages of female models with their mouths slightly open to enhance their ability to project a sexy vulnerability. That's the mouth-breather pose done deliberately, with the cultural connotation that the woman "knows how to please." (How ironic that these magazines are aimed at a fashion-conscious female readership.) Done without intent, the look still carries a cultural meaning, but it's as negative as the deliberate version is positive. The person with the mouth hanging open appears not to know anything; it is the look of overwhelming stupidity.

EXERCISE: NAME THAT EMOTION

As you watch a sitcom or soap opera with the sound off, name the emotion that the actor is trying to project. I recommend these types of shows because of the exaggerated emotions and situations that are often present. They give actors a chance to "overact," so the facial expressions will be more like those of a live theater actor projecting to a person 25 rows away from the stage.

Body and Mood

You may think you've pegged the emotion of the person based on facial expressions, but then you see arms or posture that seem to project something different. Here are a few common gestures that are either misinterpreted often, or not understood for what they really mean:

⇨ **Crossed arms**—In presentations to body language students, as well as mixed audiences in all kinds of venues, this is the gesture that people get wrong. They generally assume that crossed arms are a barrier; the person doing it is closed to you. Sometimes, that's true. But if you see a receptive face and hear openness in the conversation, consider the other reasons why someone might have crossed arms, such as:

o   They are cold.

o   They are hiding hands that are not well-groomed.

o   They are overweight or pregnant and using the gesture to "hide" the middle.

o   They are disguising very long arms or very short arms.

o   They are asserting a dominant position.

o   It is a habit.

⇨ **Legs crossed in a figure 4**—I had a journalist from *Der Spiegel* accuse me of arrogance solely because I tend to sit like this, rather than crossing my legs like a proper European gentleman. My legs do not do the latter, so I have no choice. Her judgment was projecting, which is something you always have to curtail when reading body language.

⇨ **Hands clasped in front of genitals**—Also known as the fig-leaf posture, I call it "protecting the precious." Men of all cultures do it when they feel the least bit threatened. Is it possible that they do it when they do not feel threatened? Sure, but consider that there are many degrees of threat—some of them overt and physical, and some of them subtle and psychological. Women have their own version: crossing arms tightly to the abdomen to protect their primary organ of gender.

➪ **Hands on hips**—This is often a sign of defiance, but pay attention to determine where the fingers are pointed to be sure. A man with hands on hips and hands pointed toward his crotch has definitely struck a defiant posture. His face and voice may be all smiles and deference, but this posture, especially when combined with a wide stance, means he is feeling bold. For a woman, the comparable posture is hands facing back toward the butt cheeks. When a woman faces her hands forward, it might still be a defiant gesture, but when a man faces his hands backward, this is a stereotypically gay posture in Western culture.

In all these cases, do not underestimate the force of habit and cultural differences when it comes to body language. Many of us fall into using gestures that we saw our parents use in certain circumstances and venues. The stronger the role model, the stronger the residual behavior.

Strong Messages

There are times when the signs point to an extreme: either you have won the person over, or you have failed miserably. Just as useful to you is knowing when the person is either sitting on the fence or good at hiding his true feelings.

You Win

In most cases, a genuine smile with the muscles around the eyes engaged indicates you have gotten through to someone. The person's focus is on you. You notice open and fluid illustrators, with hands and arms indicating receptivity. You may even notice mirroring of your illustrators, which shows that the person feels in synch with your ideas. At the same time you see these positive responses, but you also see signs of nervousness (that is, adaptors), just feel affirmed that you are engaging the person while you have likely established yourself as super-typical in relation to him. Watch for nodding and other regulators that say, "Yes, keep talking" as further confirmation that you're winning him over.

You Lose

You are looking for the opposite of the "you win" body language: movements that are closed, jerky, bored, and hateful. With someone energized in the wrong direction, you may see the artificial smile, obvious use of adaptors suggesting impatience—pen tapping, finger rubbing—and gestures that say "back off" and/or "shut up." Or you might have pushed your target so hard that you see the signs of abject intimidation: fig leaf; drooped head; and excessive use of self-punishing adaptors, such as cuticle picking. If you have aroused someone to the point where they are attempting to get rid of you quickly, you may suddenly see barriers such as crossed arms and legs, or the placement of books or a huge vase of flowers between you.

You Have an Undecided...or a Gumby

Some people dodge and weave so ably that you have a hard time figuring out if they have normal, predictable responses to anything. Some people just dodge and weave because they have such a hard time deciding to go in any particular direction.

With the latter type, you see raised brows and hear utterances that indicate questions. They make attempts toward openness. With the former, you get more circumspect behavior. They might ask you a lot of questions, and try to exercise control over where you meet and what time you break for lunch—all the while projecting openness and receptivity. If you are in a situation that has multiple options for him joining sides, look for signs he is vacillating between you and others. These would include divided attention: focusing on one, and then the other; sending a hidden signal to each of you; or fleeting smiles at either or both that he quickly contains while watching you from the corners of his eyes. In some cases, this is calculating; in others, unintentional as his squirrel-in-the-road brain searches for equilibrium.

Establishing a baseline for the rest of the body can be through simple observation of how the person moves, or you can make an exercise out of it, just as you did with eye movement. It's good to start with the exercise just so you get some practice in watching with intent.

EXERCISE: OBSERVE MOVEMENT

Have your subject sit comfortably, but in a position that allows movement. In other words, a cushy couch is not the ideal place. Ask questions that move from casual to personal to prying. As questions grow more and more invasive, you should notice body changes. Here are sample questions, which obviously should be recontoured depending on the person to whom you're talking:

1. *Where did you go to elementary school?*

2. *What kind of fun things did you do at recess?*

3. *Did you ever fight with the kids in your class?*

4. *Did your teachers ever get down on you for something that wasn't your fault?*

5. *What was the worst thing any of the kids ever did to you?*

6. *At some point, you must have done something hurtful to them, too. What did you do?*

7. *Have you done anything similar to that as an adult that really made you feel disgusted with yourself?*

You can take a different approach to get the same kind of result. In this case, you just keep pushing for more and more details until the person runs out of information. At that point, emotion and the stress that goes with it will surface.

⇨ What's the most exciting thing you've ever done?

o "Skydive."

⇨ Why was it so thrilling?

o "I didn't think I could do it, but as soon as I did it, I wanted to do it again."

⇨ Did you have to take a course before you jumped?

o "We were in a classroom for about two hours and then we got about two hours of practical training. Our instructors were really safety conscious."

⇨ What are the most important things you have to remember when you skydive?

The questions can escalate to a level of such complexity that only a pro or someone with a great deal of experience could answer them. When your subject reaches the point of "I don't know," or "I don't remember," and you keep asking questions, she'll probably start to feel inadequate, and might make excuses for not knowing. As the uncertainty sets in, watch for sudden changes in body position and for movement in the arms and legs that suggest that some emotion is leaking out.

Probing

Here are a few more techniques that allow you to get information without clearly asking for it. Keep in mind that they are overtly manipulative and should be used cautiously. Remember the exercise on determining what someone's strategy is as you use these techniques.

⇨ **Repeat what people say**—By simply repeating what someone says you can often get him to elaborate on its meaning, and maybe even drive him to admit that what he said is not quite true. For instance:

"I saw 80 elk on the road today!"

"Wow, 80 elk?!"

"Well maybe 50. I did not have time to count. The road was chaos. But it was the most I have ever seen. There must have been a forest fire!" In saying this, he reveals an inclination toward hyperbole, at least in one admission. At the very least, he divulges information you can use to continue to the next step. A related application is using his words to anchor a point you want to revisit. Rhetorically stating, "Wow—80 elk!" gives you a placeholder for later. It shows you made note.

⇨ **I'll show you mine if you show me yours**—An age-old spy trick. Volunteering a piece of information that seems private or confidential often begets a response in kind. (Of course you never give up anything of value.)

⇨ **Parallel questioning**—I did not put this category in the questioning section because it relies on multiple styles of questions to take someone down a parallel path to disguise your main point. Let's say you want to find out who dominated at a recent meeting of department heads because you have a vested interest in having the technology group prevail. The colleague you've cornered at the coffee machine would be happier if marketing had its way, so you don't want to reveal your interests to her.

"That meeting room was packed with chairs. Did everyone bring a date or something?"

"They invited in some management consultants to make a presentation about how to improve operations."

Eventually, the conversation yields what the consultants recommended, so the parallel lines converge.

Active Listening

Active listening means you not only hear what people say, but also what they are not saying. You can use it to uncover facets of people that would not surface if you took their conversations literally. It's a matter of using auditory and physical cues to hear and see where the passion lies. Without active listening, you might as well just read the transcript of a conversation and try to get the meaning.

People with whom I've worked have often asked me how I knew something that wasn't stated obviously, maybe some piece of information from a source or clue about his character. In my early days as an interrogator, I didn't know, and I would pass it off as instinct. The fact is that I was using active listening to hear implied messages. Often, I would hear the words that were not said the way you can see the silhouette of a familiar face and know exactly what features would be there in a room with bright light.

Active listening has another huge benefit: it forces you to pay close attention to what another person says and what you are really saying. If you're a salesperson, it might even help you dump that stupid habit of using the customer's name over and over again. That line they gave you in sales training about the most musical sound to a man (or woman) being the sound of his name? Garbage. The music to him is the sound of his own voice—so listen to it.

Most people like to talk, as long as they don't feel they are hogging the conversation. A healthy exchange is the way to get someone to divulge how he sees himself as special, or differentiated, or how he wants to be seen as special.

Clues

Verbal tip-offs that you need to pay attention to as part of active listening include:

⇨ **Making odd word choices**—Incongruous choices and push-pull words are two that set off my radar. An incongruous choice would be anything out of place for the person, such as a laid-back guy suddenly spicing his sentence with harsh criticisms of some politician that he probably heard on TV. Interrogators use the term "push-pull word" to describe a word that no one says without a reason; for example, he makes an "honest" living. That should be a given. It's akin to me saying, "I'm a real red-head." In that sentence, "honest" becomes a point of negotiation. It raises questions about what you consider honest, whether you know someone who makes a dishonest living and you want to draw a contrast, or the possibility that maybe this person who makes an honest living *now* didn't always. You could put a lot of common expressions into this bucket because they undermine the credibility of the person: She *literally* saved my life. This product is *very* unique. *Seriously*, I don't know anyone better suited for this job.

⇨ **Emphasizing certain words**—Whether the emphasis occurs in the right places or the wrong places, it tells you something about how vested the person is in the topic, and it could point to stress about the issue being discussed. Put emphasis on the italicized words in the previous paragraph and you get the sense the person is enthusiastically over-compensating. But put just as much emphasis on every word in the sentence, and you'll come up with someone who sounds desperate, angry, or some other extreme emotion. In all cases, that points to stress.

➡ **Glossing over a topic**—Sidestepping a topic or smoothly sliding around the meaning of a question to move on to a more comfortable subject both indicate the person wants to hide information. How many times have you seen a politician or other celebrity embroiled in a scandal respond obliquely in an interview? "Good question, Mike! I have a story that will illustrate where I am on that topic…," followed by a journey down the rabbit hole.

➡ **Bridging a time line**—Making a time line leap while telling a story or answering a question alerts an active listener that you have some reason to be uncomfortable with the topic. It's a perfect set-up for a lie of omission. "Sorry I'm late. I met with the client all morning and then came straight here for the meeting," might raise eyebrows if the client's office is two blocks away and the meeting he's late for is at 3 p.m.

➡ **Switching to passive voice**—This is a great way for someone to put distance between himself and a topic; there could be lots of reasons for doing this. One might be fear of punishment, like the little kid who says, "The Richardson's had their window broken while we were playing ball." Translation: "someone hit a ball through the window, but I'm not telling you who did it." It could also be a way of muting the pain that an active retelling of an event would bring: "my brother was murdered." The passive way of presenting the information softens the statement and avoids sharing a stark description of a brutal killing.

⇨ **Shifting cadence**—When people get excited, they tend to speed up a bit. Shifts in cadence can suggest a lot of the other conditions, too. Maybe the person has some uncertainty about the subject matter, forgot exactly what he was going to say or couldn't find the right word, or really wants the subject to go away.

Interpreting these clues will be a lot easier when you combine your auditory perceptions, knowledge of body language, and facts about a person you can extrapolate through reliance on "guilty knowledge."

Guilty Knowledge

In addition to those clues providing insights into the person's state of mind regarding a topic or situation, you also need to apply skills in detecting what interrogators call "guilty knowledge." The phrase makes particular sense in the context of a criminal investigation, in which a suspect might describe elements of a crime scene in ways that only the perpetrator would know. For our purposes, a more generic term might be "private knowledge."

In a bar in Atlanta, I once overheard a woman ask a man who was flirting with her to "say again." That's a military way of saying, "Repeat." After that, it was comfortable for me to approach her and say, "How long were you in the military?" I've also recognized a hand signal between two people at a meeting that ground troops use to communicate "cover me, I'm f*#$ed." Once something becomes a pattern in your subculture, and you find yourself in conversation with people outside it, you give guilty knowledge of being part of that subculture.

While filming *Guantanamo Guidebook* for Channel 4 in England, in the course of the simulation, I ordered a "guard" to get the prisoners out of their stalls. The guilty knowledge in that would be obvious to a small group of people. Interrogators might pick up on the fact that I did not say "cages," which is the term we use for the prisoners' cells. Horse people would pick up on the fact that I used a term with which they are familiar. An interrogator with any experience in the horse world would know immediately that Hartley is a horse man.

Most people have no idea they are dropping hooks such as these during their conversations. In a first meeting with a business contact based in Wisconsin, I heard a melodious North Carolina accent. I remarked that not only was it a pleasant surprise, but I could pinpoint exactly where that accent came from. That led to a very friendly conversation about my being stationed in North Carolina. In a matter of two sentences, we realized my job had put me 200 yards from her grandfather's farm. Imagine how that accelerated the bonding process. When I spoke, her ears were open.

Someone could have done the same thing to me after hearing me drop the word *stalls* in an exchange that had nothing to do with horses. Without even making reference to the fact that I said it—in fact, it would be more subtle without that— he could mention later during a cup of coffee that he'd just taken his first riding lesson. That would catch my attention quickly and give him the positive response he aimed to get.

Whether it's an accent, a speech pattern, or a regionalism such as "pop, "soft drink," "soda," or even "Coke," to refer generically to a sweet carbonated beverage, people leave clues all over the place about where they're from. Similarly, the clichés people use give you guilty knowledge. I have a friend who calls pilots "bus drivers"—typical Marine Corps slang. Metaphors will often give you insights as well. In meetings, I've sometimes said, "I feel like a hog with a wristwatch" when I don't understand something. You probably will not hear a New Yorker come out with that one.

Now that you have some knowledge of active listening with your ears, let's do it with the body. Once you get what people are saying or are not saying on an auditory level, you can draw some firm conclusions about them when you observe.

Mannerisms, posture, energy, focus, the way people sit or stand, and so many other pieces of body language come into play as well. Remember the Big Four and how they signal emotions: illustrators, regulators, adaptors, and barriers. Illustrators punctuate thought, for example, but what about giving away guilty knowledge? Within minutes of meeting a senior executive of a company I worked for, I said, "How much martial arts training have you had?" Raising his eyebrows, he told me about his black belts and wondered how I knew. His physique signaled fitness, but I combined that with the fact that he stood squared off with me as opposed to standing oblique, which is the posture most men adopt unless they're being confrontational. Just like oddities in speech pattern, oddities in body language or positioning indicate guilty knowledge and past experience. Stay aware so you see the indications of how someone is different relative to you and others in the group. When you see this difference, drill down, and keep in mind that these tools are double edged. Just as others leak, so do you. Pay attention and take note of your own guilty knowledge.

The Tools in Action

This true story, which leads to a positive experience for both parties, illustrates the way that the various tools, especially active listening and guilty knowledge, contribute to the bonding process.

Anyone from any walk of life can show up in places such as Home Depot and Lowe's. I was in one of them looking for particular woods for a project, and had almost no flexibility in what those woods would be. The projects I was working on dictated precise selections. Pine was not a good choice because it's brittle; it can fracture and shatter. Other woods had other deficiencies in terms of my outcome, so my remaining choices were elm, ash, and beech. Beech was the ideal choice, but it's very difficult to find where I live.

In frustration, I abandoned the wood section and went to pick up a tool. A man who looked like he might be early retirement age walked toward me and seemed curious about my interest in the tool. My body language—smile, nod—signaled openness. He said, "Tried one of these tools before?" I told him I had, but the one I tried wasn't very good, and I needed some accessories to do what I wanted to do. "You woodwork?" he asked with a glint in his eye. "Not really. I'm more of a crafts guy. I build things," I said.

In just a few sentences, I knew he understood lumber. He used terms such as "navigate the wood," which told me he did something that required manual dexterity in addition to the right tools. And so I asked him, "What's your hobby?"

"I'm a carver."

"Oh, really," I said in a kind of upbeat way. "I have a friend who's a carver." Shortly after, I inquired about the kind of wood he uses, and he suggested it was a little bit of everything.

A little more chat and I got him to describe the cartoon characters, cowboys, and other small figures he carves, and what wood makes the best choice for each. He impressed the heck out of me and I soon thought, "This guy would be fun to know more about."

As the conversation drifted into the subject of something his son had just made on a wood lathe, I told him that I use a wood lathe.

"What kind of wood?" he asked me.

"Ash." His eyes lit up, so I followed that with a question: "Know where I can get some?"

"You bet I do," he said.

As we continued to chat, I soon found out he had a bunch of 2×12 beech slabs, and that he would sell them to me for a reasonable price.

He lived close, so we made arrangements for me to go to his place and get the wood. I also put him in touch with my friend, Rick, who is a carver.

EXERCISE: TOOLS FOR A GOOD OUTCOME

Go back through the list of tools I discussed in this chapter and see how many of them came into play in this real encounter.

Think of everything here as a toolbox, much like the woodcarver's toolbox. You need a plan for which tools get you to the next step. If you start with a file when you need a saw, the outcome will not be so good. But if you use the tools in an orchestrated fashion and in the order they are needed, the results can be remarkable.

CHAPTER 5

Human Modeling

You are about to study animals in their natural habitats. Think of yourself as a keen observer similar to Jane Goodall, only with the ability to speak chimp.

The process of human modeling that you learn in this chapter will help you understand both strangers and people close to you in a particular way—a way that gives you the information you need to influence their behavior. It will help you create a holistic view of the person that highlights needs and motivations.

I cannot overemphasize how important this modeling ability is. By pinpointing key traits of a person and seeing whether they are strengths or weaknesses, ordinary or extraordinary abilities, you get a clear picture of the person you are going to manipulate. Bypassing this step means you might get lucky and hit his hot buttons or find something relevant while you are in the process of trying to manipulate him, but your outcome will be unpredictable. You're just shooting in the dark. We start every interrogation with as much knowledge of the individual prisoner as possible; this includes information gleaned from those who captured him, and those who feed him and manage his daily life. We then go into the interrogation and ask questions to add more detail to the picture of who he is. This picture presents the peaks and hollows in his personality, so we know what he has in common with us, and what his advantages and fears are. Without this knowledge, our efforts to manage his sense of belonging or need to differentiate could have disastrous results.

The tools in this chapter are designed to give you another sense of sight into a human being—an understanding of the person as he sees himself, as well as how others see him. It is an investment worth making. Only if you are capable of reading someone's mind can you forego this step.

You will use the tools you just learned in Chapter 4 to learn information relevant to drawing a detailed map of the person you have targeted. If you're good with the tools, then you will have a pencil sharp enough to draw the details. These tools also come into play once again as you interact with the person to get him to do what you want.

Your first step in sketching the map is to admit that you do not know everything there is to know about your target. It doesn't matter if the person is your mother, a colleague you've worked with for 15 years, or your best friend. There are facts you do not have about that person that may be extremely important in influencing her behavior.

EXERCISE: NEAR AND FAR

Make a list of three people you hardly know and three people you believe you know extremely well. For each one, list what you think is the dominant attribute;, for example, intelligent, devout, artistic, hospitable, sexy, judgmental, and so on. For each one, list what you think is the person's dominant need; for example, respect, acceptance, adulation, forgiveness, and so on.

After you finish reading this chapter on human modeling, come back to this list. Consider occasions that will allow you to use your new tools to verify, refine, or negate your initial assumptions.

The Personal Operating System

According to Wikipedia, here's what an operating system does: "Performs basic tasks such as controlling and allocating memory, prioritizing system requests, controlling input and output devices...." Humor me here: Imagine that a person's thinking and behavior is driven by an operating system. That operating system is running on hardware defined by genes. Only certain programs will run and some will run differently than they do on someone else's hardware or operating system.

In order to examine this operating system, you would need an MRI (magnetic resonance imaging). That MRI would show you engrams corresponding to portions of the brain a person uses when she engages in a particular kind of thought. Because you cannot see this, you have nothing to go on but the intangible indicators. How is that different from a Mac or PC? Like the difference between MS Windows and Mac OS, there are tremendous differences in the way people operate, regardless of the biological similarities. The way the person interfaces with the world and specifically other people is, in that way, analogous to the way an operating system functions in a computer. This operating system dictates priorities, information handling style, and reaction to new input.

When we discuss human beings, how information is processed is beyond our scope. By the time that book is written, the material will be dated anyway, because MRIs are changing our understanding of humans on a daily basis. So here, I want to concentrate on how a person reacts to things in the outside world. I find the easiest way to discuss this is in terms of overarching behavior patterns. I will arbitrarily call these "personality types" for purposes of our discussion here.

Personality Types

Similar to any believable book on people, this one does not give you a comprehensive list of descriptions of human beings. You need to look at your individual target, who just may inspire a whole new category. People are an amalgamations of genes (hardware) , experiences (programming), situation (input), and hormones (power surges). Not one of these can be overlooked when understanding a person. So take this rudimentary system I've laid out here as a set of suggestions, and baseline your target to figure out exactly what he is.

These personality types are like operating systems only in that they have bearing on the person's perception of input, priorities of processing, and how information is handled.

In an interrogation, we always establish control and rapport, and our success in doing so quickly is contingent on our ability to codify the source's "operating system." We base this ability on mechanisms built into the military scheme: We have guards, cameras, and microphones to ensure there are no private moments in the compound. Your needs for information about your target are no different, even though your techniques for getting it are. You need a grasp of your target's attributes, habits, and state of mind. You need a sense of the continuum of all things that never change for him, as well as the elements that shift around on an ongoing basis.

Each person has an over-arching personality type that remains consistent for long periods of time, if not throughout his mature life. What I'm giving you is just a sampling of contrasting types. You should use this as a springboard to creating your own lists, which will likely reflect your own culture, ethnicity, nationality, and so on. For now, start by understanding each of these personality types and how they contribute to your efforts in modeling a human being. In later chapters dealing with the application of skills, I return to these types so you see how to tailor your strategies and tactics to get what you want out of each. That will provide the examples and structure you need to customize your efforts to influence someone who falls in a category not covered here.

These pairings can be visualized on radial diagrams. As you go to the extreme in one, you approach the other, just as you've probably observed in political systems. The most important reason to understand this is so you can get the insights related to self-image that you need to manage and predict outcomes. If your actions challenge your target's self-image, your ability to move him the way you want depends on knowing whether you'll meet with avoidance, rejection, acceptance, or a total system crash.

Pretentious Versus Earthy

Pretentious people are shaped by their insecurities. They look for a model of life that is acceptable, if not superlative. The pretentious will try very hard to impress those whose opinions matter. In terms of the most pretentious types, everyone's opinions matter. If you have ever seen a single episode of the long-running sitcom *Frasier*, you picked on the comic premise that Frasier's (Kelsey Grammer) posturing about art, cuisine, wine, furniture, and music all come from his desperate hope that his tastes really are more refined that anyone else's. And his brother, Niles (David Hyde Pierce), has no hesitation about either reinforcing Frasier's judgment when it alleviates his own insecurities, or attacking it if taking Frasier down a notch will make him feel better.

Truly earthy people are simply content to be who and what they are, whether that means they have gray hair and wrinkles or dated furniture. Earthy people feel comfortable with their own rhythm in life. Others may not agree with them, but the earthy type remains indifferent.

On a radial diagram, the earthy type can go so far that the gray hair, thrift store clothing, and tie-dyed couch covers are defining and displayed for their own sake. When this happens, the laid-back elements become inviolable parts of life, and the image of earthiness simply becomes another kind of pretense. In many cases, fashion trends, and even lifestyle trends, grow up around what starts out as earthy, but it is quickly co-opted by the mainstream, pretentious crowd. A few years ago, this surfaced with a dramatic rise in the cost of outdoor clothing as a few trendsetters adopted the gear of the earthy—the stuff you used to get at gun shops and army–navy surplus stores—and made upscale, sport-specific clothes desirable for people who never came near those sports. The so-called "green" fashions, now the rage on the catwalks, are another example.

On the opposite extreme, the pretentious can go so overboard with differentiating that their behavior becomes bizarre, pushing so far to the edge that they are removed from society. Their eccentricity moves them past the point of pretentious as they become unconcerned with the opinions of those who "do not matter," so they, in effect, become earthy and quirky in their indifference to mainstream opinions.

The reason the extremes matter is this: If you plan to get a pretentious person to do something, you need to understand how that person perceives himself in the bigger picture. Does *your* opinion matter to him? How does he perceive himself in terms of the others in the group you are interacting with? Is he so pretentious that he believes only the opinions of those "in the know"—with whom he has only voyeuristic contact—

matter? You need to understand how he processes input and prioritizes information to understand how to best interact with him.

Similarly, if the earthy person is so indifferent to what people think, how do you appeal to her? Can you talk down to her (because she just doesn't get it) and expect anything to change? You need to act on the understanding of how rooted and fully integrated this personality type is to ascertain whether the person is moving toward esteem or trying to belong. This will influence your decisions about how you help her to differentiate or belong. For instance, the pretentious may be moving around the bend and getting so close to earthy that a few simple disclosures would make him appear eccentric. Knowing that, you can ask questions and make comments to move him there with ease, or at least to show him you're capable of doing that, and then rescue him in exchange for a favor.

Pretentious　　　　　　　　　Earthy

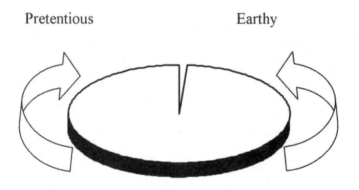

Balanced

Conforming Versus Anti-establishment

Conforming people find their comfort in being part of something. They try to fit squarely within the group. They may express opinions, but the range of them will be dictated by what falls within a normal range for the group. The idea is similar to national party politics: you can have radically different opinions, so long as the rest of the party embraces them. These people follow the rules because rules matter; they keep the world in order. The resulting insulation is centering.

For them, a tremendous sense of security emanates from feeling part of something through this behavior, and they bolster that feeling and refine their self-image by avoiding any deviation from it. Follow this to its logical conclusion: The conformist gets so close to a specific issue that he loses sight of the overall picture and begins to differentiate to the point of divergence. At that point he becomes anti-establishment. Some gun-rights activists fit this type. While the right to bear arms is sacred to any soldier, it can become so entrenched in some people's psyches that they become the harshest of anti-establishment types.

Anti-establishment people eschew the rules, think structure is for those with no imagination, or believe that there is a better way than what has come to be. They believe that, if the right person were making the rules, the rules would be better, so, in effect, they are simply advocating another set of rules. What if they had their way and suddenly the rules were different— in fact, exactly as they wanted them? When antiestablishment types get so caught up in the rules that they start mass movements, they cross the line. They move to become the establishment. When they are in charge, they become more conservative and conformist in an attempt to hold onto their sacred idea.

When an idealist is the enforcer, he simply cannot imagine that his idea is wrong; the problem must be in those who are enforcing it. Look at the great reform movements of the 20th century for governmental models of idealist turned conformist. In most cases, the definition that comes from being anti-establishment is a dramatic attempt to seize power and establish a new order for its own sake. These people make great followers for the insidious, aboveboard leader.

In practical application, you need to understand whether your target conforms for its own sake, or strikes back when he had no voice in the decision. This understanding gives you the opportunity to manage his drives. If he is a conformist and you want him to do something, the easiest way is to create a coalition and move him along with the room. Coalition building is much easier than direct conflict. By altering the group norm you will easily move along a conformist. After all, he either moves or becomes an anti-establishment type. When differentiating him, his drives will be to become a more solid participant in the group; when he is sufficiently differentiated as to no longer belong, he will need a new place to "belong." Belonging is powerful.

If he is an anti-establishment type, let him in on "the vision" and how you plan to do things. If you can make him a true believer, he can become a soldier in the cause. Simply understanding the psyche of the anti-establishment type allows you to target him as well. Most anti-establishment types believe there is a better way. Once those people truly become invested in the outcome of the group and stand to lose, they rarely continue to stir the pot. To paraphrase the social author Eric Hoffer, people with Happy Meals and Cable TV do not revolt. Causing the anti-establishment guy to belong squarely in the group and allowing him to "change things from the inside," you co-opt his passion and create a soldier for the establishment. You simply have to remember to tend his fire or he will stagnate and become an opponent.

Know-It-All Versus Guru Seeker

The know-it-all takes bits of information, whether relevant or not, and applies them to the situation. In many cases, he does this by relying on the fact that he has been "more right" than others in the past (like my 5'3" friend, who was taller in the past). Despite the fact that he may actually know more about some things than others, his need is to know more about all things than all others. Not surprisingly, the know-it-all gets wound up when he meets someone who may actually know more than he does. Whether it is because he went to a better school (or simply lived near Princeton or Harvard), has more experience, or just "knows the business" better than you do, you encounter this type commonly in the workaday world. He is an archetype; he is Cliff the mailman on *Cheers*. This type's sense of belonging and esteem comes from the deference he receives from others for being a font of information. That shapes his very identity. In some cases, he doesn't suffer from intellectual narcissism, rather he is insecure and well aware that he is full of crap, but hopes secretly that others do not notice. By using the tools described in Chapter 4, you can probe to determine which state is true for him and plan accordingly to move him farther up or down the Hierarchy.

The guru-seeker wants enlightenment from an approved source to claim the validation as his own. No amount of knowledge, performance-based achievement, or success will give this person the same amount of joy and validation that quoting the maharaja will. He needs to know that what he is saying comes from an enlightened one. The danger for this type is that gurus can comes from all walks of life and how trustworthy his guru is depends on his selection criteria. The guru may just be a know-it-all who has been elevated by deference of others and, by using the snowball effect, has leveraged himself to guru status. On the other extreme, if the guru seeker fulfills his needs and gets continuous validation from the Wise Ones he approaches, he can get to the point where he looks down on others who have not shared the presence of the guru.

A practical example of this is an acquaintance of mine who worked for the group promoting Buckminster "Bucky" Fuller's work in sustainable and renewable technologies. Fuller, best known for his design of the geodesic dome, had died by the time this person got involved in the work, so he obviously never even met his guru. Nevertheless, the gospel according to Bucky ruled his life and nearly everything that came out of his mouth. A common response to people who criticized him was, "Bucky was a genius. You wouldn't understand."

When a guru seeker gets to this point, he begins to understand the world according to his guru better than anyone else. In effect, he becomes a sort of demi-guru, as he feels justified in enlightening lesser beings. In effect, he can serve as the guru's gatekeeper to ensure that, although the path is wide, the gate is so narrow that few can pass through it.

Demonstrate to someone with cockeyed confidence in his facts that he got something wrong and one of three things will happen. First, he gets defensive and dances around the mistake, very likely trying to maneuver you into thinking that you misunderstood. Second, he crashes through the floor of the Maslow level he's on—maybe reputation—and now seeks nothing more than belonging. Third, he becomes aggressive and attacks you, but probably not on the same point you challenged. You tell him what he said about elephants is wrong and explain why, and he lashes out that you dropped out of high school. That's exactly what this Bucky-adoring acquaintance does, and, as a result, he has to move quickly from one circle of "lesser beings" to another.

Understanding where each of these fits in the Hierarchy will help you determine a best course of action. Based on several factors, his personality will dictate whether that information is valuable and actionable. These factors include: authority of the source, deference (in both directions) with the source, and style of delivery. It is often easier to get concession from a know-it-all when he is allowed to incorporate the new knowledge into his lexicon, so asking leading questions and letting him divulge the importance of what you know fits his style of understanding without resistance.

With the guru seeker, establishing yourself as one to which he should be deferred, or quoting Nostradamus-like prophecies, will get you further than blurting out facts. Think about evangelists who don't offer a single fact or personal insight, but win people over by quoting the Scriptures. By establishing that your knowledge is simply borrowed from a sage, you get more approval than trying to say you are the guru. Guru seekers only follow those with a following...until they get that they can be nothing more than a messenger.

Traditional Versus Trendy

In the extreme, both are first cousins to pretentious. This has more to do with how people are grounded than what their tastes are. Do they need the approval of past heroes to validate their choices, or is the opinion of super-typical humans alive today good enough to override the judgment of generations? The interesting piece is how caught up in trends some people can become and still label themselves "traditional." Social pressure is powerful.

I once had a traditional friend who touted the everlasting supremacy of classical music. Because it had survived for hundreds of years over its contemporaries, she said, it was clearly worth more than modern music. I pointed out that Culture Club CDs can theoretically survive as long; she conceded the point.

Traditionalists trust the known and believe that things have evolved the way they have evolved for a reason. Whether they realize it or not, they espouse a belief that the accidents of history involving groupthink are more profound than the groupthink of today. The outward appearance of the group is to lean on traditional means of dress and trappings of authority, to lean toward old ways of doing business, of etiquette, and even of eating. When others adopt corporate casual, they stick to the high end, wearing starched shirts and slacks instead of khakis and golf shirts.

The extreme of trendy sees the current opinion as weightier than grandma's. For those of this group who put conscious thought to it, the argument is that this generation knows more than all past generations—perhaps because of our accumulated knowledge—and is, therefore, in a better place to make decisions. Superficially, their focus seems to stay on what's hot right now and adopting the latest trends. In the extreme, they think about the long-term outcome of what they are doing today, because everyone else is doing the same thing. A trendy activist might (ironically) protest against tearing down a historic building because every other trendy person has it as a priority activity. Behavior such as this provokes the traditionalist to ask, "If everyone else jumped from a bridge…?"

Traditional and trendy, then, are more than statements about fashion sense or preferences. Trappings such as clothes and decorations illustrate how someone sees her role in a particular environment. The traditional person openly declares that what has gone before has value, and part of how she demonstrates her own value is by carrying on tradition. She is a guardian of history, a promoter of classic looks, sounds, and smells. A hard-line traditionalist may not be able to get past differentiators such as tattoos and tongue studs to connect with a person.

When taken to the extreme, one begins to look like another. Taking tradition to the extreme can become a trend and negate the original purpose of the movement. Few people understand where traditions come from and how convoluted they have become through the years. Taking a tradition and following it *ad nauseum* can result in trendy behavior, because the supposed tradition is nothing more than a thinly veiled attempt at creating a trend. Look to pundits on the far left and right politically to see the practical results of this confusion: they both pull out the sacred traditions of democracy as sound patterns for action while they laud "change" as the only answer to our problems.

Trends can also become so ubiquitous that they become the tradition; and generations later, no one is the wiser. Tattooing as an indicator of individuality has long since passed the point of breaking with tradition, and now could be seen as a badge of belonging instead of a badge of differentiation with society. So we have to ask ourselves: in five generations, will tattoos on the small of the back be seen as standard for old, staid, politically conservative women?

In dealing with either type, keep in mind how each perceives her relationship to the organization as she is persecuted as *avant guard* or respected because she is old school, or vice versa. Either extreme affords you unique opportunity to manipulate feelings of belonging and differentiation, but you must first understand how the barely belonging 18-year-old employee fits before attempting to differentiate, or else you will isolate her.

Justified Versus Open-Ended

Justifieds and open-ended thinkers are related to traditionalists and trendies, and you can probably see how many of these other sample categories show similar relationships.

Justifieds populate the extreme wings of churches and political parties, but they even show up in companies in the form of people who insist on something like six sigma as the answer to all corporate woes. They are people who live in a politically liberal enclave who say, "Just because you're a Republican, you don't understand this," or people of a given religion who feel so much pity for an atheist that they hound him with Bible verses. The justifieds feel as though they have every reason and every right to preach their version of correctness—and they often make logic-driven people a little nuts, and very angry. Right about now, you may be thinking of all those justifieds you know and feeling superior about your balanced points of view. But think about something that escalates your passion every time you think about it, something that you believe contributes enormously to the quality of your life. Maybe it's books. Would you act like a justified if the publishing industry suddenly decided that all books should be in digital format only?

Extremely open-ended thinkers have the "anything goes" mentality—no fundamental rules to life. Everyone should be allowed to do what they want within the bounds of…nothing. This group fits the Ayn Rand objectivism model. These people believe that the Christian Fundamentalist movement, which so quickly passes judgment on homosexuality and children out of wedlock, is skewed and wrong.

They also point to the intolerance of the whole system, and that things must change and people must be allowed to live as they wish. In healthy doses, this means liberty with no intervention by religion or government. Unfortunately, the extreme expects the government to create a church-limiting process, thereby interfering with the beliefs of the religious extreme. When this happens, the government is telling religions what their dogmatic constraints are. The result of moving so far to the open-ended is that the open-ended thinker becomes a justified in the way he does business.

Of all the groups I've covered, these are the two most closely related because at their center is the basic belief in the freedom to believe whatever you want to believe. Ironically, it takes very few steps to go from open-ended to justified and back again. Approaching either of these types unprepared is risky. Use questions to explore how the person sees himself. Steer clear of areas where the person has hot spots, except to demonstrate he is irrational and fracture him from the group.

— — — — —

Your ability to peg the operating system gives you the first key piece of information you need to get a specific person to do what you want.

If you're familiar with other systems of describing personality, you may have a tendency to question how these categories—and I want to reiterate that they are samples, rather than a comprehensive list—relate to the Myers-Briggs Type Indicator or the Enneagram System. First of all, these two standards are both valuable ways of gaining insights into human personality by applying certain evaluation criteria. They will tell you something about how you relate to the world, as well as to certain situations.

My purpose in coming up with this "system" of contrasting types with common-sense labels is twofold: (1) to point out how extremes of all kinds eventually come together and, therefore, can be very similarly influenced; and (2) to focus the discussion on self-image, and the factors that molded it and sustain it.

In his book *The Power of Risk*, Jim McCormick came up with evidence from surveys that supports this notion of extremes meeting at a point, but he puts it in the context of strengths and weaknesses. His Strength/Weakness Paradox states "Our greatest strengths and weaknesses are one in the same. All of your strengths have the potential to become weaknesses." In short, any positive trait, if applied in the extreme, can become negative. (p. 49, Maxwell Press, 2008) Take any of the previous categories that you immediately perceive as positive and follow it to its extreme, and you will get the negative. The persistent search for a guru turns a curious person into a know-it-all. The zealotry of an earth mother will turn her into someone extremely pretentious.

Clearly seeing each of these for what it is will allow you to predict how the person will collect, process, and prioritize information. While most people will live somewhere on the continuum closer to the center, finding someone who is close to the edge allows you a prime opportunity to nudge them in the direction of someone to which they see themselves diametrically opposed—and that push followed by a retrieval may be just what you need to get what you want.

What Makes Johnny Run?

What exactly did this person decide to load onto his "system"? And once the programs are loaded, where does this person excel? What does he do in a middling way, or where does he fall below the norm? Which of these things causes him pride, and which shame?

Understanding all of the aspects of the character, all the factors that affect self-image, can tell you why the person behaves the way he does, and where he has areas of strength and weakness. Once you plot the information about each trait on your mental bell curve, you put them together to compose a 3-D image of where this person is average or typical, where he falls below the norm, and where he stands out above the crowd. This visual representation allows you to define the whole person relative to others in the population with which he identifies.

Let's look at a well-known celebrity from a distance and talk in terms of what we can see without getting close to him.

What do you know about John Travolta?

You may consider yourself a big fan of his work, and even know a few non-movie tidbits such as his love of flying jets and involvement in Scientology, but could you draw a complete picture of the man? Here are facts you may not know that puts flesh on the skeletal view you have of this celebrity:

⇨ Siblings: six.

⇨ Family religion: Catholic.

⇨ Education: high school dropout.

⇨ Early career: recorded about 20 music singles between 1969 and 1978.

⇨ Other career: author of a children's book and a fitness book.

⇨ Children: a boy and a girl.

⇨ Causes: human rights, education, health education, children, animals, environment, and gay rights.

When you look at the whole picture—and there is obviously a lot more to know about John Travolta—you see that he is typical in several ways (married, two kids, family size somewhat typical for a Catholic Baby Boomer-era family). As an award-winning actor, singer, dancer, and author, he might be called super-typical. Dropping out of high school at age 16, however, makes him sub-typical in the American culture.

In short, how you classify John Travolta in terms of his relationship to other age 50-ish American males depends a great deal on which part of the picture you are shining the spotlight.

Taking just two characteristics, here is where John Travolta would sit on bell curves:

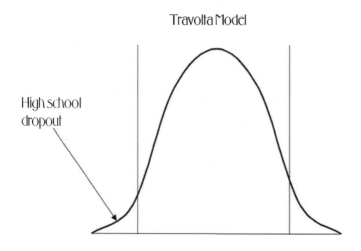

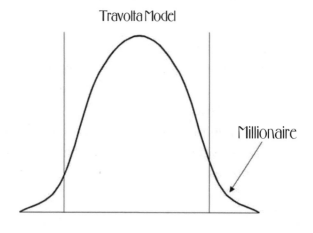

The first illustration shows Travolta being among the 15 percent of U.S. students who dropped out of high school in 1970—obviously sub-typical. Then, you complete the bell with the percentage that graduated and the percentage that went on to college that year.

The second illustration shows Travolta being among the 8.9 percent of Americans who are millionaires. Compare that with what middle class is in terms of income, and how poor is defined.

The Old Bell Curve: How Typical Are You?

In the past, I have often used a bell curve with students to represent a range of values so they see how their experiences and characteristics can be visually represented as typical or atypical. I might ask:

"How many of you have cut your finger with a knife at least once?" Everyone raises their hands.

"Twice?" Most keep a hand up.

"Five times?" A few hands remain.

In this model, anyone with a finger sliced less than twice is sub-typical; two to five times is the norm; and more than five times is super-typical.

Although it's a distorted view, it does capture one fact about this group, made up of these particular people. People who cut themselves more or less than the norm, for example, might see this as a springboard for conversation at the break. Why? People seize on commonalities and differences to create taboos and create bonding.

Any of us can be typical, sub-typical, or super-typical, depending on the environment and circumstances. Steve Jobs is super-typical in the greater understanding of American culture. An able-bodied 25-year-old man who lives with and is supported by his parents is sub-typical. A 45-year-old woman who processes loans at a bank is typical. Are there aspects of American culture in which Steve Jobs is sub-typical or a geek? Sure. This helps us to better understand why demographics and statistics can be used to make any point we want to make.

In this model, the super-typical reign. The typical, wanting to be more like the ruling class than those "below" them, allow the super-typical to influence their behavior, tastes, and other aspects of their lives. The typical admire and even emulate the super-typical in the hope of gaining their approval. Meanwhile, the sub-typical look up, hoping to become typical. If you want a clear example of this, just look at the way kids group themselves in high school.

Our primate cousins in the ape dominion behave this way. The super-typical comprise the ruling class with the alpha-male by establishing a pecking order in which he is king. The others jockey for position. The pack includes the super-typical alpha-male and female, the masses, and the sub-typical, but the last group is barely part of the pack. Human beings replicate this model on different scales.

As a rule, humans emulate the super-typical of their group. Look around at the people in your workplace. If your boss—the person able to promote you, endorse your plans of action, and authorize a Christmas bonus—wears a suit to the office every day, you will probably emulate that style in the hope of boosting her approval of you. Does the latest trend started by super-typical Celebrity X spark spin-offs in the population, regardless of whether it's a fashion trend or one related to behavior or speech? You may think you are immune, but try to hide from certain ubiquitous facts about celebrities that creep into the most serious conversations, such as: Tom Cruise is an active member of the Scientology community. Britney Spears was taken to a psychiatric facility. Heath Ledger died suddenly at the age of 28. Celebrity watching thrives with a billion-dollar industry serving the intellectual curiosity of pop culture geniuses.

The New Bell Curve: How Unique Are You?

Through the ages, experts have developed all kinds of tests to give humans concise ways of describing each other. The Myers-Briggs and Big Five systems offer ways of characterizing personality, emotional intelligence (EQ) tests give you a sense of how well you perceive and handle emotions in relation to the rest of the population, and intelligence quotient (IQ) tests supposedly tell you how smart you are. All of these tests have serious limitations, though. For example, intelligence tests evaluate a very narrow band of ability, which is why I find them almost useless in evaluating someone's real intelligence. This is like evaluating someone on the basis of a series of flat bell curves to determine what's normal. The evaluation itself has no relationship to what's normal, only to what is the norm for a particular group.

A person can reach high levels of esteem and a fantastic reputation at work, or through activities that have nothing to do with work. The first is the person who has a career, or at least a job, that energizes her. She cannot wait to demonstrate day after day how competent she is because she loves the work. She may go home to a TV and peanut butter and jelly sandwiches every night, or she may go home to a vibrant, loving family. The second is the person who makes a living doing Job A today and Job B tomorrow, and then spends evenings and weekends focused on a completely different activity. This is the actor working as a waiter, or the competitive skydiver working as a barista. How would you know what the other half of the person's life is like unless you know her in both settings?

If you looked at either of these people in a single dimension, you might see a person who is not fulfilled. And you could be very wrong.

With every person you want to influence, you want more than the information from the flat bell curve. You want to ask the questions that reveal depth, so that all sides of the bell take shape. Your job is to find where they are super-typical and stroke their ego, or if you are using a negative approach, find their weak spots and offer to help them up from subtypical. Knowing their unique combination of character traits and abilities is the information you need to get them to do what you want.

This is what interrogators do: work people in places where they feel strong, as well as in places where they feel weak.

I have a friend named Libby who has been perennially underemployed since we met about 15 years ago. A wonderful actor—acting is her passion and her "night job"—she generally takes receptionist jobs with few intellectual demands and very set hours. If I were her boss and wanted Libby to do something for me at the office, I would get nowhere if I focused on her role in that work environment. She wouldn't do a damned thing for me. She would just quit and move on to the next receptionist job and I would never get what I wanted. In tying incentives or pep talks to her day job, I would demonstrate that I was oblivious to her priority: being on stage. But if I invested the time—and it isn't necessarily much time—in knowing what she does with passion, I could talk to her. I could articulate the reasons why homing in on certain parts of her day job could help her be a better actor; then I've caught her attention and got some leverage with her.

At its core, this approach is about respect for the whole person. The image of the bell serves as a visual reminder of the advantages of doing that.

Most people are balanced. If they are really strong in some areas, they are weak in others, because human beings have only so much bandwidth. The key is finding out which things cause them pain, and which add value to their lives. In trying to capture the role of Elizabeth I, whom most of us remember for her grand successes, Cate Blanchett summed up how she tried to capture the holes in the queen's persona in an interview on *www.50connect.co.uk*: "What I have tried to do in this film is to create a sense of a hollow woman—without a companion, a husband, a child—searching for what replaces that void."

For most people, their 3-D bell would not be a pretty one. They would have parts that bulge to show their prowess, and parts that sink to illustrate their incompetence. There would be dings all over the bell. The tools I'm giving you here allow you to easily see those dents and bulges. That's the knowledge you need to manipulate someone's behavior. On rare occasions, you will see the more solid bell of someone whose capabilities are not great, and neither are his shortcomings. He is truly balanced. This "ordinary man" will be your toughest case.

Why the 3-D Bell?

Bell curves provide an excellent visual representation of relationships between bits of data. This means a single snapshot of how Johnny relates to Becky in terms of numbers of fingers and toes, siblings, and so on. So if all I look at is the number of children in the family and income level, I get one picture of a person. If I look at the arrest record, I get another. Just like the brief analysis of John Travolta illustrates, a complete picture of a person integrates lots of different traits into the image.

The model of a bell curve I'm introducing here attempts to take the same approach. For example, look at the results you get by representing a person as sub-typical, typical, or super-typical in a dozen different areas. Overlay the curves on one another in a 3-D way so that you can theoretically walk around it and look at all the sides. This is the kind of model you need to create for your target. When you do this it is like creating a topographical map of who the person is. The visual allows you to understand where he feels pride, strength, weakness, or shame, and where he feels normal or average. More importantly it allows you to know about the areas where you can *make* him feel these emotions.

You will not be able to determine when a person has reached the pinnacle of his environment or when he needs to be lured beyond his environment—both of which are fundamental to getting what you want—unless you have a more robust model for assessing someone. You have to see the person holistically so that you can know reliably where he is strong, weak, and average. In short, how balanced is he?

By coordinating multiple flat graphs into one 3-D representation, you get an image of the person that looks like the Liberty Bell. You might even imagine cracks in the bell in areas where your ostensibly superhuman target shows subpar performance in certain areas.

As I said, interrogators stroke a person's ego in spots where he is strong, and push on him to the point of pain in spots where he is weak. You will do essentially the same thing, but I want you to begin by visualizing it in a way that has more relevance in business settings and other aspects of daily life; that is why the 3-D bell is useful.

⇨ Step 1: You need to look at the myriad lines that make up your subject's bell, and see where he sits.

⇨ Step 2: You will use the tools described in Chapter 2 to move him along that line—to a more super-typical position, to a more sub-typical posture (if you choose a negative approach), or to a different bell curve entirely. The latter is a result you want to effect when the person has reached the absolute pinnacle of the bell curve.

⇨ Step 3: You now have him in a position to "close the deal," a process that I describe in the next section.

To show you how Steps 1 and 2 *could* work, I'll go back to the profile of John Travolta. First, here is how selected traits look on bell curves that could be overlaid into a 3-D image:

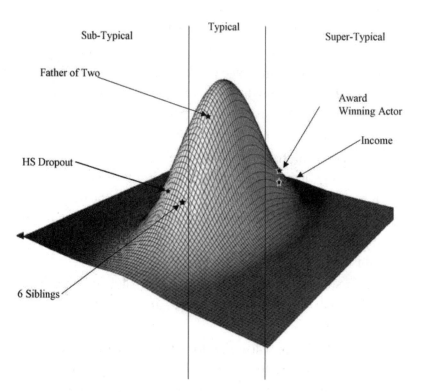

With average Americans as the group

If you wanted to gain leverage with this award-winning performer and highly accomplished pilot—nearly at the pinnacle of the categories of movie actor and amateur pilot, respectively—you might look to his causes. What could you do to raise his profile as a human rights advocate or a champion for the ethical treatment of animals? Using the positive approach to getting someone to do what you want, your action to move him into the realm of "super-typical" *among celebrities* within those causes may give you some unique influence with him. I say "may" because I use this solely as an example of how this process works, not how it would work specifically with John Travolta.

In an office setting, you could potentially do this with the CEO by targeting her causes, and then presenting her with an opportunity to give the keynote at a fund-raising event for that charity. Another approach—one that a friend of mine took—was to focus on her boss's love of physical fitness and invite him to be her guest at a health club with trainers that could take you to the "next level." She got a lot of lunch invitations from him after that, as well as a Christmas bonus.

The exercise of profiling a person with the level of scrutiny required to create a 3-D bell curve may have some surprising results for you, too. You may realize or discover something about a person that gives you a different perspective on working with him. You may decide that a respectful approach aimed at bonding feels more natural than pushing him away, or vice versa.

The reason why someone may look well-balanced in the 3-D bell is that they compensate for ranking super-typical in some areas by being sub-typical in others. The illustrations related to John Travolta hinted at that. Look at that mix of achievement and underachievement in other people you know well, either by reputation or personally. Thomas Jefferson, for example, not only served as the third president of the United States, but he also distinguished himself in fields such as horticulture, architecture, archaeology, paleontology, literature, and education. He was far less super-typical in his personal life: his wife died after 10 years of marriage and he never remarried; of his six children with her, four either died at birth or when they were babies. In short, he could devote most of his prime years to everything but home and family. Most likely, if you work in an large office, you have come across at least one person who works overtime voluntarily and excels in production, but has no one to go home to, or doesn't care to go home to whoever is there.

You know more about the areas where someone like that is super-typical, because people typically lead with the edge they want people to see. So when you see someone who projects an almost super-human amount of achievement, look for areas where he is an underachiever. And many times the most balanced people will not be overachievers in any particular area, because they go through life doing little bits of lots of things.

As you mentally plot a person's 3-D bell and the span in super-typical areas seems enormous, you need to keep probing to complete the picture. They will likely be just as broad in sub-typical areas. They excel in other things and pay for it somewhere else.

Creating the Bell

I told you that interrogators collect information with guards, cameras, and microphones, but because you don't have them, you'll need magic. That magic is the adept use of the tools covered in Chapter 4. In this section, you will exercise them in building rapport, baselining, and gathering information, so you can create that 3-D bell of your target.

Apply these techniques inconspicuously. You will get resistance ranging from a skeptical look to harsh expletives if you pry and push for information. That means you should start your conversation broadly and allow your source to direct which questions you ask. Don't gut your plan at the outset by asking your boss, "So, what makes you tick?" or, "What really embarrasses you, sir?"

Much of how your target responds will be driven by his operating system. If you asked a pretentious type what he is most proud of, you can guarantee he will offer an answer—a complete one. He will likely also take the opportunity to answer the same question by giving you an anecdote about swimming with crocodiles and losing his keys in the Congo. On the other extreme, you might find a well-adjusted earthy type giving you a sarcastic answer and asking you why you care.

So keep your collection effort to typical conversation with two differences. You have a mission, and you are the one driving the conversation. These are the steps you will follow:

1. Establish rapport.
2. Establish baseline.
3. Understand the threshold.

4. Gather information.

5. Reinforce rapport.

Establish Rapport

This bridge called *rapport* can only join people who have something in common. That could be something as simple as age, or shared misery with the workplace. Or it could be something unique, such as a love of Italian sports cars. All the subject will do is serve your desire to start a conversation without it seeming contrived.

Establish Baseline

Listen for his stress-free style of word choice, cadence, pitch, and tone. Look at his body language and eye movement patterns in casual conversation. Note anything that you might consider a glitch that's normal for him. It could be something subtle, such as a certain way of using pauses, or it could be something you find decidedly odd, such as focusing to the side of you instead of making eye contact.

When you know what is normal, you can see abnormal. As you start the conversation, you detect cues in body language and hear clues in his stress of words about what is important. Using active listening skills founded on his baseline, you can know what is a source lead; you follow it and make the conversation flow naturally. If you fail to use source leads, your style of follow-up will seem wooden. He may suspect that you're probing, which will trigger an instinct to resist.

Understand the Threshold

When you work in the bodyguard business, you are taught to use a technique called *threshold braking*. This involves riding your brakes to the point that your car is slowing, but there is no perceptible dip to the nose of the car. The reason you learn this is because it allows you to steer as you brake, which is vital in maintaining control of the vehicle at all times.

As you ask questions and follow his leads, think of the threshold-breaking metaphor. You pay attention to signs that he feels you are probing. You do not want to push to the point where you see a reaction. The only way you will be able to spot and adjust to changes in mood is to ride the brakes with no perception that you are braking. Any indicator that he is starting to sense you are doing more than chatting means you have to transition immediately to a less-threatening topic. Loop back to something innocuous that he mentioned previously.

EXERCISE: FIND THE THRESHOLD

You can do this one with someone you know well, or someone you will never see again. Pick a hot topic. Talk to the person in broad terms and work your way toward that hot topic. As you start down the path, watch and listen for indications that you are getting close to an emotional reaction, but consistently stay just short of it.

> *If the person is a good friend, break and debrief him on what you are doing. If the person is a stranger, break and talk about something positive. Pay attention to news interviewers as they take this approach. Notice that sometimes they cross the line, and you can see the response in their source brewing before the explosion. Do not get to that point with your source.*

Gather Information

As you follow the conversational leads, appeal to his pride. Flatter him when you've clearly entered an area of pride. You will see similar indications in a male or female—chin up, erect posture, perhaps shoulders broadening, and clear enunciation with a bit more volume and excitement in the voice. Pinpoint the accomplishment and stroke his ego to get him to give you more detail. Buried in that detail will be other links that will allow you to follow up using good questions. You will readily be able to find out things, such as why he is so proud of this particular accomplishment. Maybe he beat the odds. Maybe he turned around one of his biggest-ever failures.

As you gather information, pull out all kinds of tools from your toolbox. These will get you some quick results:

⇨   **Repeat words.** Repeat words you want him to give
     you more information about. Humans naturally

drop words we want to talk about, and are more than willing to educate those who do not understand the things we are passionate about. Prey on this natural tendency. Follow his conversation style and talk about what he wants to talk about, but anchor places to which you want to return by repeating that word along the way in conversation and keying his mind to return to it. If you use the word out of context he will need to fix that for you.

➪ **Rely on the useful sisters: flattery and criticism.** By using these levers, called *pride-and-ego-up/down* in interrogator terms, you can lever behaviors as part of the conversation. Asking "what were you thinking when you did *that*?" is a mild form of criticism that will likely elicit more details than he normally would divulge. The same is true of flattery. People feel the need to be understood, and will clarify when you show them you don't understand. When you are seen as a kindred spirit, they will give you more of a good thing.

As your 3-D model of the person takes shape, you grow to understand both the individual and how that person fits into the various groups to which he belongs. He may be ordinary at work, but a hero and leader among the Shriners. Focus on the former, and you could miss his real grounding, just like most of the people who work with my actor friend who is perennially underemployed in her day jobs. By knowing to whom you are talking, you can motivate your target on a level that matters deeply. You won't just pay lip service to his needs and desires if you get this holistic picture based on information you gather both overtly by asking questions and covertly though observation.

Reinforce Rapport

There should be no pressure in these exchanges—only information collection. These steps are about understanding your target, not manipulating him. As you progress through the conversation and ease of it, remember the role of emotion in reinforcing rapport. Regardless of how excellent someone plays golf or sings, the objective opinion of that skill isn't nearly as important as the emotion the golfer or singer attaches to it. We have all seen celebrities crumble in the public arena because they *felt* they fell short of a brilliant performance, whether that was in a sport, a movie, or a concert.

You can plot someone on a bell curve, therefore, and not get a true picture of how that sub-typical, typical, or super-typical status in a performance area affects her self-esteem or shapes her aspirations for self-actualization. This is the subjective information—the color and texture of the image—that enables you to reinforce the rapport you have built.

Enter the Prototypical

In reading about all of these types of people, whether related to status in a group or extremes of behavior, it may have occurred to you that something is missing. These are people similar to John F. Kennedy and Princess Diana on a grand scale, and someone for whom you had huge admiration in your community or even your family, but thought they were out of reach.

You might quickly conclude that you do not know anyone personally who fits this description, but that's probably not true. Did you know anyone in high school who you felt was destined for greatness? Someone whose success did not bother you, as in, that person was not your rival, but somewhere above being your rival? You may have no idea where that person is today, but your positive memory of her is sacrosanct. All of us have known people like that at different phases of our lives, and in different positions. It's almost as though they are a different breed of humans.

These are the prototypicals. Once a person becomes prototypical, he is not part of the culture anymore. You would never put them in your class. They are like a new class of being: human, but not human in the way the rest of us are.

The Greek gods are classic representations of the prototypical. They are people, just a different class of people. According to mythology, they manifested pettiness, anger, irrational behavior, romantic love, and lust just like humans, yet they had superhuman powers that made them worthy of the adoration of an empire. What's the difference between them and Princess Diana? Not much.

We have a constant need to look for figures such as these who are better than us, but a persistent need for those people to be one of us. We look for ways to bond to them. The more prototypical they are, the less we rejoice in their destruction. And yet, as we've observed with many heroes of recent times, it is possible to have such a fall from grace that the prototypical status can never be regained.

The best example of that is probably O.J. Simpson—from football and movie star to the possible owner of a bloody glove—although Michael Jackson and Elizabeth Taylor are also good examples. Elizabeth Taylor was Hollywood royalty until she married Senator John Warner. Going to political fundraisers instead of the Academy Awards is a great way to put yourself down a few notches in the eyes of most Americans. Michael Jackson probably never stopped being a musical genius, but when allegations flourished that his genius was accompanied by perversion, his stature also plummeted.

When prototypicals such as this fall, those who viewed them as having an almost godlike stature are likely to go through stages of grief as Elisabeth Kübler-Ross described in her book *On Death and Dying*: denial, anger, bargaining, depression, and acceptance. Why do people care about the fate of someone like O.J. Simpson—as though it is a form of death? We do not want them to fall because, if they do, what can happen to us? When someone like O.J. Simpson goes through a series of legal traumas and shameful behavior, we feel "wrong," because we have been worshipping the wrong "god."

The social dynamic involving a prototypical person differs from that of "normal" people. For example, the fearless leader of your company who commands respect by walking into the room may have a lousy golf game. The fact that he shoots three times his age does not bother him in the least, though.

He has nothing to prove out there, and will continue to command respect—even on the golf course—just because his persona is that of a prototypical person.

You are probably thinking, "Life must be sweet if you're prototypical." Not nearly. You still have the basic human need for peers, only you find yourself surrounded by people who see you as peerless. That can be an incredibly vulnerable position, as many prototypical people who have forged questionable relationships have demonstrated with disastrous, exploitive marriages and business partnerships.

No matter where the person is on the bell curve, if you are using a negative approach to getting what you want the key question is: How do I make that person feel as though he is losing his grasp on belonging? The belonging could be company, club, circle of friends, or even family. It's not even belonging in an absolute sense. It's belonging in the sense of what he perceives his role to be in that group.

The Who and How of Your Target

Is the person you have targeted to influence capable of giving you what you want? If not, what *is* that person capable of in your grand scheme? Help or detriment?

Once you determine that an individual is capable of fulfilling your desires, you can lay out a plan for accomplishing your objective. That plan begins with the exercises in human modeling to get an understanding of the individual's core personality type, as well as his status in his group. As you progress, you might suddenly find he is not the right person to give you what you want, but rather someone who is instrumental in getting the right person to do what you want. The modeling exercise gives you the information you need to progress forward in a new direction.

As you model people, do not wear your dark glasses, or rose-colored glasses, or whatever kind of screen that customarily distorts your vision. Projection of intent, motivation, and human qualities that are born by need will destroy your ability to understand someone. You will be a victim of your own prejudice, stress, and emotional baggage if you let these factors filter your perceptions of the person you have targeted.

You need to do the same thing in his group. You may have a tendency to inflate the value of his group—something such as Mensa, for example—or to ridicule it, depending on your point of view. Put that aside, because your assessment of the group's value is not the critical factor: you need to know where you target fits in the hierarchy of his group. Someone who reigns as super-typical in an unusual environment has achieved success and gives him a kind of security: he has met the need for belonging, advanced to having a sense of reputation and status, and may even have achieved self-actualization. It is those bare-bones factors that give you the information you need to manipulate him.

This phenomenon applies in any context. Whatever it is, the group provides a chance for a person to belong, but it also offers opportunities to excel. Your ability to model someone depends a lot on whether you look at him in the context of the group, whatever it is, and leaving behind your assessment of whether not the group is worth belonging to.

Once you have collected salient details of your target's personality and place it within the Hierarchy, be cautious. Handle that knowledge carefully, or you will damage the person's psyche. To get what you want, you may need to show your target that it *can* happen, but it is rarely beneficial to do so.

SECTION III

Applying the Tools

CHAPTER 6

Bonding and Fracturing

Bonding and fracturing enable you to exploit the two big needs of belonging and differentiating.

In terms of the Hierarchy, the need to belong falls just under the need to achieve status or reputation; that is, the need to differentiate. Much of what you will be doing in exercising influence, therefore, will be moving people up and down the tiers.

You will find most people stuck between floors on Maslow's Hierarchy. They ascend a few stairs and then self-sabotage, taking them back down. Sometimes another person or even a whole group sends them back down by locking the door to the next level. This is how interrogators work: they establish control over the ascent and descent, as well as the doorway to meeting higher needs. This is also the model for how you will work. Through bonding and fracturing techniques, you either reinforce a sense of belonging and further differentiate someone as super-typical, or reduce a person's distinction and even place his sense of belonging to a group in jeopardy.

Talk With Intent

You begin by simply talking to people—with intent. What you learn in conversation will enable you to model your target, grasp the dynamics of the group, and then use tactics to bond or fracture. Talking with intent means probing, planting certain questions, active listening, and reading body language. It creates the opportunity to use psychological keys, such as flattery or criticism.

Believe me, the first thing that will happen when you converse with intent is that your human interaction will deepen. It may sound as though I'm asking you to treat people like zoo chimps, but that is exactly opposite from what you should, and need, to be doing. There is nothing inherently wrong with knowing what makes someone tick; in fact, it's the kind of information that marriage counselors try to get clients to reveal to each other to improve relationships.

At the same time, there can be a Machiavellian quality to using the tools of which you should be aware. Intelligence officers of all stripes use some variation of them to extract information. You need to know how that works, too, because as I said in the very beginning of this book, manipulation is part of the program.

Many of us with the U.S. military during wartime have served side-by-side with allied soldiers. We are close with our allies, with whom we have an enormous amount of trust, and with whom we share a great deal of information. But not everything. Regardless of the open relationship, soldiers of different nations can be too open. Allies collect information on American operations and Americans know it. Unless we decide to share a government, we will not start sharing certain sensitive information.

The problem we in the intelligence field have encountered is that young American soldiers often get so caught up in who they are talking with that they forget what they are talking about. This is the way that spies get information from people who should know better. Whether it's a woman trading sex for secrets or a jovial host sharing schnapps with a foreign national, they make you forget who they are. They bond with you. After that, they pare your options, which is a process I explore in depth in Chapter 7. In brief, after you feel as though you belong—you are in the hierarchy to which this person belongs—then that person makes you feel special. You are differentiated. You may feel as though he thinks you're the only one worth talking to, or you're the only one worthy of making love to her. After that, it's a small step to making choices that keep you in that person's company and eliminating options that remove you from that person's company.

The technique does not sound so exotic when you realize that it happens in offices every day. Moving from bonding to putting someone in a compromising position happens in sales meetings, board meetings, interviews for jobs, client presentations, and myriad other business-related activities. You can do it with strangers in a business environment as easily, and sometimes more easily, than people you see on a regular basis.

Here is how I might launch a conversation with intent, use some key tools to model and bond, and then achieve my outcome of finding out information useful to a pending negotiation. I show up 20 minutes early for an appointment with Bill Smith, a prospective client. My objective is to find out something salient about the character and interests of Bill Smith, so that I have some leverage in our meeting. I greet the receptionist with a simple, "I'm really early. Please don't bother him for at least 15 minutes." I pick out something that tells me what's important to her or what may be a source of pride: "You have a wonderful speaking voice. I'll bet you spend your evenings on stage." That will either get a yes or no, but there's a good chance the comment will be followed by a little more insight into her interests and personality. I move the conversation about those interests to the office: "Do people at the office know you're a star?" And after, I find out that rehearsals sometimes dig into office time. "Bill Smith strikes me as the kind of CEO who encourage employees to do what's important to them"—a comment that might elicit raised eyebrows in surprise; a knit brow that says, "Are you kidding?"; or maybe a big smile and nod that broadcast "absolutely." Regardless of the subject of the conversation, if I find out whether or not Bill Smith treats his receptionist with respect and support, then I find out a lot about his workplace priorities. Does he care about having her feel as though she belongs? Does he do anything to give her a sense of status? Does he support her efforts toward self-actualization through this very important "night job"?

Knowing how he tunes into the needs of employees will give me clues as to where he himself sits in the Hierarchy of Needs. More importantly, if he is doing a poor job, and I can identify his needs and fulfill them, then we bond and information flows freely as he forgets who I am.

Engage With Intent

Bonding and fracturing are ways to dismantle a person's drive, and rebuild it in the way you need it to take shape—to draw the person toward you—but that process only makes sense if you have a defined outcome in mind. To clarify the importance of this point, I want you to focus on the difference between a bully and an interrogator.

Even though the two rely on very different skill sets, you wouldn't know that if you watch a lot of bad TV. Ask someone who has only seen depictions of interrogators on those melodramatic crime shows to mimic an interrogator, and he will try to intimidate the source. This is not what makes interrogations work. What works is to get into that guy's world and look out—to move to a position inside his head so that we understand his point of view. That is the point of the psychological keys, or approaches, that I described in Chapter 4.

Children use some of these tools instinctively to cajole or coerce their classmates and siblings to comply with requests, give up information, or, in some cases, just to watch other kids squirm. When children do this, they prey on natural drives and sensitivities. As we grow up, two things happen: we are forced to stop behaving like children, and we begin to realize that others have value. We also run out of time to focus so much energy on other people. Our senses dull to the possibility of getting people to do what we want.

Many of these skills you learn in this book are grown-up versions of kid's games such as teasing about big ears or ugly shoes, and then relieving pressure by changing the subject. Fishing to find out secrets is another big one. The tools of interrogators, therefore, bear a striking similarity to things kids do naturally, but the childhood skills are put to sleep as life gets in the way.

The adult version of tools does have a significant difference: the application of them relies on cognitive thought based on knowledge. How you use these tools and where you start is dependent on your understanding of the complexities of human social interaction, not what you can get away with.

A bully walking into a schoolyard always picks on the wrong stuff, which is generally the most obvious flaw or weakness—flat feet, big nose, skinny body, red hair. We all recognize that pattern of the kid who takes on other kids just because he can. Bullies are unsophisticated. At the same time they realize the power associated with separating someone from the crowd, they fail to do it well, and usually can't follow through with any meaningful action.

The only time an interrogator like me has leverage with a source is when I personalize the attack. I do not mean personalize by telling the guy that he has big ears and red hair. He's probably looked in the mirror recently and already knows that. Unlike the bully, the interrogator personalizes it by bringing something to the forefront that the person really wants to guard. That creates anxiety. The offer to relieve that anxiety in exchange for the person doing what I want puts me in a position to extract useful information.

A reverse use of the skills is to take the awkward girl next door, befriend her, and pump up her image so that she becomes as popular as the beauty queen. In short, I can make you nothing or make you hot with the same set of tools.

It's all about the intended outcome. A good interrogator probes to find out what music makes the person dance, and then moves backward to make the person dance toward him. The action of influencing that person is an ongoing process of implementing your strategy to lure him toward you. Sounds a bit like seduction, doesn't it? Think of interrogation, then, as seduction, and bullying like rape.

An integral part of an interrogator's success, unlike a bully, is the balance of threat and rescue. Whereas a bully wants only to threaten, an interrogator embeds a sense of potential rescue to keep the source moving toward him. The reward of cooperation—of performing the right dance—is that the threat will stop.

Act With Intent

As schemes of influencing human behavior, bonding and fracturing require coordination. They sound like opposites, but you will often use them in concert to achieve an objective.

Here is an overview of how bonding and fracturing may play out with your target:

⇨   Bond a person to you.

⇨   Bond a person to the group.

⇨   Fracture the person from you, but bond him to the group.

⇨   Fracture the person from the group, but bond him to you.

⇨   Fracture the person from you and the group.

This last one is not useful in terms of getting someone to do what you want. It is the scenario that interrogators scrupulously avoid with a valuable target: threaten to pull the rug out from under your source, but never actually do it. If you follow through with separating him from everyone, then you are left with an individual who has faced personal extinction, and no good has come of the encounter. The only exception is if you can artfully reverse the trend and help him to belong again, but with a much weaker perception of personal power.

The Dynamic of Bonding

These stories point to the two primary reasons why people bond:

1. Common enemy.
2. Common cause.

The Arab saying "any enemy of my enemy is my friend" points to the number-one way to get people to bond: give them a common enemy. Find one or create one.

Common cause may have less clarity in people minds, and different people may view the cause very differently (democracy), but it still operates as a unifying principle.

Even if there is no authentic common enemy, by creating artificial stress, you can draw someone closer to you. You see this in offices all the time, even if the effect lasts only for a single meeting or a single day, when someone points out that "the boss is in a bad mood."

Here's a real story, with the name of the lousy teacher changed, which illustrates how a common enemy can give life to a common cause.

The entire class of college-bound students thought Charlie Baldwin was a mean-spirited fool. Even the guys who played on the basketball team he coached to a winning season did not like being around him. Worse yet, in trying to teach American history, he illustrated that his grasp of any subjects other than jump shots and free throws put him in the sub-typical category among teachers. Within weeks of school starting, he emerged as the common enemy of the smart kids—most of whom actually wanted to learn American history. In a move that hardened his stature and led to his "transfer," Charlie gave Tom the Geek a detention for correcting him on a basic fact about the Constitution. Mary, a prissy bookworm, blushed as she stood up and said, "I will take detention with Tom."

This led to the entire class volunteering to take detention with Tom, which led to a sudden rescinding of the order for Tom to stay after school.

This is a microcosmic view of what has happened in civil rights protests, anti-war demonstrations, and workers' strikes. They all had faces of common enemies: a man in Ku Klux Klan white, President Richard M. Nixon, Sam Walton. The common causes embodied in the vision of a common enemy brought protestors to their feet and moved them to focus their anger somewhere specific.

Bonding a Person to You

What binds people together who have nothing more in common than going to the same college? It's not necessarily a matter of common experiences; it's more likely common thinking. You may have had the same negative professor for a physics class, and that shared opinion of him would give you a much stronger bond than just sitting in the same classroom.

You can use your knowledge of this to project the image of a person you know someone wants to see and relate to. Essentially, through your conversation, you create a person who does not exist by bringing forth a role that gives the person something familiar to latch onto. I once had a dialogue with a reporter who was from Youngstown, Ohio. I've never even been there, but I used to live with a girl who grew up in Youngstown. I mentioned that, and the tone of the interview changed markedly as we "shared" perspectives on the challenge that Youngstown faced after the collapse of the steel industry there.

The more familiar something is, the more it will evoke particular kinds of responses. It could be positive or negative, but when it's positive it can accelerate the bonding process. Every one of us has memories, both factual and emotional, from previous relationships and situations, and they are the genesis of prejudices of which we may not even be aware. They can manifest themselves in odd ways, such as the dislike for an actor because of his teeth, or the desire to be close to a woman who just happens to look a lot like your favorite elementary school teacher.

When you perceive that someone is inexplicably drawn toward or repelled by an individual or situation, you can use that to either fuel the momentum or put yourself between the person and the perceived "threat."

This bonding factor, even as flimsy as it may seem in this example of the reporter from Youngstown, can cause people to divulge secrets to a stranger who really doesn't care about them, as opposed to someone they know better who might actually be sensitive to their situation. The assumption is that if they have some particular thing in common, it grounds the relationship in a way that makes that person a worthy confidante.

Discretion is a sophisticated skill requiring intelligence. When someone blurts out a secret or carefully takes you into her confidence, you need the ability to respond in a manner that reassures the person that you understand your responsibility. At the same time, unless you know the person extremely well, that individual who entrusted you with the sensitive information will likely be walking on eggshells, hoping that you don't tell. That gives you power—power that evaporates the instant you do tell.

In short, common ground leads to a bond, and your discreet respect of the exchanges related to that bond glue someone to you.

Bonding a Person to the Group

You could have two different dynamics at work here. First, your target might want to bond with the group, and by making that possible for him, he owes you. Or, he might have no reason to bond with that group, but you make it necessary or desirable for him do it, thereby getting what you want.

The first involves a classic quid pro quo. By belonging to a group where you have influence to get him in, he achieves not only belonging, but also status. What he gives you should put you even higher on the Hierarchy, maybe something that helps you go from enjoying self-esteem to pursuing self-actualization.

The second scenario is more complicated. It's the one that field operatives use to recruit agents, so you can look at the strategy in both a positive and a negative light. First, the negative.

Why do young people in the U.S. military commonly become Palestinian sympathizers after they study Arabic at the Defense Language Institute? They are bombarded day in and day out with language and culture studies that differentiate them from most other Americans, who cannot understand Arabic and have no exposure to Arab rituals and traditions of Arabs. It's natural to be drawn to a body of information, and even a population, when you know more about them than anyone else. You identify with them. It's a phenomenon that has played out time after time with CIA agents such as Philip Agee defecting to Cuba on moral grounds. If you get too close to the enemy, you start to sympathize.

Interrogators have only a "secret" clearance, as opposed to the higher "top secret" clearance, because they have a job requirement to understand the enemy's point of view. We talk with them every day, for hours at a time. By nature, we have to be empathetic in order to get them to talk, so we start feeling what they feel. We start to smell, talk, sound, and eat like the people we live with—the prisoners—because we mirror, and there is a real danger of getting too close. It's possible to get drawn into a vortex and not be able to get out.

To varying degrees, a version of this plays out in businesses all the time. The most common is clever ad campaigns, which convince consumers to join the group of millions who would never use any deodorant but yours. Or, you invite someone who does not want to make a deal with your company to do something with your group that provides a reason to bond. In the mid-to-late 1970s, this is exactly how Bergdorf Goodman CEO Ira Neimark wooed a string of top Italian designers to his store—on his terms. After staging extravagant shows for some designers, others wanted the leverage to have their designs featured in a similarly high-profile way. But they couldn't do it until they joined the Bergdorf "family," which required exclusive relationships. They agreed, and played a key role in Neimark's grand plan to put Bergdorf Goodman at the top of luxury retailing.

Regardless of the impetus, and regardless of whether you are bonding with a friend or an enemy, one fact reigns: The closer you bond, the harder it is to refuse to give someone what he wants. The more sensible the request, the more likely it will be grated.

These students at DLI sympathize with the Palestinians without a single request from Arabs to become sympathizers. The genesis of the bond is that their native Arabic speaking teachers have become friends, role models, mentors—and occupy super-typical status in the students' world.

In some cases, bonding with a group can also represent differentiation of some type. For example, the Arabic professor thinks Gary is the best student he has seen in years, and Gary truly understands his people, so Gary has huge incentives to move down the path to bonding with people who ostensibly have nothing in common with him in terms of culture, religion, or ethnicity.

Peer-Group Manipulation

The DLI students who become Arab sympathizers arrive at that state on their own, but a journey like that results from deliberate action when you manage the process of making the person feel as though he is belonging by becoming part of your peer group. You know that the affectation of belonging rests totally with you. But as soon as you pull away, then he has no group to which he belongs. You see high school kids do this unintentionally by deciding to sometimes hang around with the unpopular geek. The geek gets isolated from his own peer group by virtue of association with the "cool kids," and he might even do favors for them unsolicited. But when that latter group gets tired of him or simply moves on, he's left alone, having made the ultimate sacrifice—his former peer group.

Consider how this model can even apply to someone as high profile as Britney Spears, the daughter of a building contractor and a grade school teacher who grew up in a town of about 3,000 people where the average income is roughly $17,000. After winning rave reviews for her work as a singer and dancer, earning a Grammy, and setting sales records in the music business, what did she have in common with anyone back home? Nothing. Her new peer group had to be similarly successful people. After losing her appeal by ratcheting up her image as a self-absorbed, drug-addled party girl, she had to find a new peer group—not a different group of hard-working, talented professionals, but similarly wealthy, self-absorbed, drug-addled party girls. Where could she go from there when the beautiful people moved on to more "meaningful lives" after jail and/or rehab? She was alone.

The Dynamic of Fracturing

Fracturing is the downside of differentiation: pointing out how someone is different from you or from the group, but in a negative way. Nonetheless, you can use it to achieve belonging, as well as separation.

In seeing how it can lead to belonging, consider the kind of relationship that representatives of management might try to establish with a labor leader in a union negotiation. A tactic of fracturing that person from the group could be part of an effort to make her feel as though she has more in common with management than labor. They aim to undercut her authority entirely. By differentiating the labor leader to the point where she no longer seems to have anything in common with the group she represents, they woo her into the fold, thereby gutting the mass movement. They send the message: "your capabilities make you eligible to rise above these peons." Not only is this what a good labor negotiator does, it's integral to how the Dark Lord of the Sith lured Anakin Skywalker to the Dark Side. In one quick move he fractured the young apprentice from his group of Jedi knights and instantly bonded him to the Sith, preparing him for the ultimate request.

Fracturing the Person From You, but Bonding Him to the Group

In one of my law school classes, I became incensed when a professor used a flawed argument to back a shy, young woman into a virtual corner. Being older than the other students, and equipped with a soldier's attitude to defend and attack, I cut into him with a version of "that makes no sense." The shift of the feeling of the class toward her corner and away from the professor was palpable.

What if he had done that deliberately because he knew she was an outcast, that everyone knew she "only got in because her daddy's a trustee"? That maneuver demonstrates how throwing a wedge between you and another person has an intended outcome of bonding her to the group.

Fracturing the Person From the Group, but Bonding Him to You

When you emphasize how much you and a person are alike, you can use fracturing to bond by insulating him from others, so he feels the need to cling to you; for example, if someone in your office is a real goofball with whom no one really likes to spend time. He knows this, and so he does his job just enough to keep it. You need something extra from him, though, so you point out commonalities that draw him to you. He will feel as though he has a reason to bond with you, and could never get reinforcement or honest respect from the others. He goes the extra mile for you because you make him feel he has real value.

Another version of isolating is to make the person feel as though he has no belonging to the greater group. Maybe you make him feel like an idiot in front of others, or push him in a position to alienate others. It's a dark, negative thing to do to someone, and you can potentially do it to anyone, including the head of the company. It's a dangerous ploy, but it can be effective if the person is already somewhat isolated from the group. It's a two-step process: first you drive him away, or farther away, and then, to get him to do what you want, you dangle the carrot of acceptance. You are effectively demonstrating your own power within the group by doing this; you are a force to be reckoned with. You see this play out all the time in movies. It goes something like this: Nobody likes the football coach. The guy on the bench who wants to get into the game gets dates with the cheerleaders for the top players so the guys "owe him one." Ultimately, the only way the coach can get those top players to do what he wants is to let the guy on the bench get his wish of playing in the big game.

During the time when I taught at the SERE (Survival, Evasion, Resistance, and Escape) school, I once effected this kind of isolation with cookies. One day, I walked in to interrogate a student assigned to me only to discover he was a buddy of mine from the Old Guard. My challenge was to make him feel like a prisoner who had just been captured by the enemy and now faced interrogation. Of course, his reaction—even though we were role-playing enemies—was a look of recognition and a demeanor that broadcasted that he was glad to see me. I had to stick to the rules; in this situation, my role of enemy interrogator required that I stay stern. He thought he had me and, I am sure, felt relieved. I gave him a handful of cookies just before leading him back to the compound. He stuffed them in his mouth and I could see that he thought, "Greg is taking care of me." He was still chewing when he got to the compound, where I pointed to someone else and said, "You, come with me." And then I turned to my old buddy and said, "Thank you for that information, Comrade." That had the desired effect of driving a large wedge between him and the rest of the population, because they thought he had just exchanged information for cookies. It completely isolated him. At that point, he hated me, but had no option except to talk to me in my role as enemy interrogator if he wanted any conversation with a human being.

At the end of the course, he had tears in his eyes when he looked at me and said, "That was the cruelest thing anyone did to me in the whole course."

My job had been to get him to understand what prisoners go through, and I never could have accomplished that with him thinking that I was "just Greg." In this case, I didn't think I could accomplish the full effect without this kind of heavy-handed trickery.

You can do this to some degree in daily life, and follow it up by getting someone to do what you want just by creating a situation in which you are the one who both creates pressure and relieves it. In some cases, all you need to do is demonstrate that you have the power to separate the person from the group without actually doing it. The looming threat gets the job done. The fact that you don't go all the way paints you as somewhat magnanimous; he owes you one.

Fracturing the Person From You and the Group

I began by saying that you shouldn't take this approach because it will get you nowhere with your target, but the exception is this: your target may be a group, not a single person. No matter how you look at it, however, the action ranges from simple rudeness to mean-spirited behavior, and a group that responds to it may not be a group you want on your side. Here's how I could have done this once, but I resisted the urge. One of the guys in my body language class, which is often populated by highly intelligent and skills special ops people, showed early on that he was a smart-ass. At one point in the class when I was just about to ask a question, I saw that one of his fingers was jammed way up his nose doing some serious digging. If I had called on him immediately, all eyes would have turned to him. In an instant, he would have fallen off whatever pedestal he'd been standing on. Even if the class had decided I was sharp for doing that, it would not have gotten me any worthwhile outcome, so I resisted the temptation.

All of these skills are simply pry bars to allow you to create links and divisions you can later exploit. Used for their own sake, they are overt bullying. Used correctly, they are chess moves aimed toward an outcome. When you use these correctly, you are planning every step with the good of your longterm objective in mind—the way I tricked my friend at SERE school. You decide: will you bully, or only use the tools when there is a longterm outcome in mind?

CHAPTER 7

Mechanics of Bonding and Fracturing

While the techniques of bonding center on finding commonality, the mechanics of bonding are ways to create and spotlight that commonality. So you might think that because the techniques of fracturing center on pinpointing differences, the mechanics do that as well. True statement, except that the mechanics to bond or fracture fall into the same categories. The outcome you get is a matter of how you use these ways of relating to people. Think of each one as a magnet: depending on where you point the magnet, it will either attract or repel.

The categories are:

⇨ Illustration.

⇨ Isolation.

⇨ Association.

Before I explore those, I want to take you through some exercises with the 3-D bell, and then introduce you to a skill set of paring options that you will use with illustration, isolation, and association.

Making the 3-D Bell Work for You

For any given person, a model displaying the characteristics of her in a 3-D format will show that commonalities exist between her and various others in a group. Susan may be a mother of three; Jack is a father of three. Both work at your company. Both have bachelor's degrees. The human brain is designed to find patterns, and it finds them well. We bond with those who have what appear to be like skill sets, tastes, beliefs, and experiences. But we are typically woefully inadequate at finding the real differences, because we habitually project what things mean onto others. Jack is a bit more adventurous than most of the other bank employees, and plays paintball on weekends with a bunch of college kids. They often stop in a local bar for a beer after games. Jack talks candidly about his college days with his young friends; he has more interests in common with these kids than his coworkers. Everything goes well and predictably for Susan, Jack, and their bank colleagues until one day someone discovers from his paintball-playing son that Jack was once arrested for possession of marijuana. The resulting chaos creates camps that break out along familiar lines: traditionalists, earthy people, justifieds. This example merely highlights the fact that, if you ask enough questions of those around you and then share the answers, you will be surprised at how different most people are from what is superficially evident.

While the overall shape of the bell is the same—at least in some places—there are anomalies. The more superlative someone is in one area, the more likely he is lacking in another. People who may appear to be lackluster because they don't stand out in any specific place may be solidly differentiated in so many others. These balanced personalities may be overlooked in a starstruck group.

By visualizing the full bell, you know what the person's drives are, and can use the tools to your best advantage, whether negatively or positively. You can take the fact that Jack was arrested for marijuana possession at face value, and contribute to his disintegrating reputation at work, or by knowing more about him, point out that his volunteer work at the high school gets kids into constructive outdoor activities. Or in a reverse situation, you can take the fact your neighbor speaks seven languages as cause for deference, or make it known that the reason he has been fired from jobs on most continents is that his Chinese is really bar slang. The holistic bell helps you to understand where to apply levers to fracture the man from the group, or bond him and add value to him as a member of the group.

Paring Options

Do not treat paring options like a party game. This is the darkest section of this book, and at the very heart of why interrogation is so demanding on practitioners as well as prisoners. I have tried to think of positive applications of this skill. I cannot. The only positive related to it is outcome; the skill itself remains negative.

Think of this harshest form of manipulation as a way to force someone to choose between two options: bad—what you want him to do that is tied closely to his needs; and worse—what he wants to do. The latter is worse, because you have structured it so that choosing it will move him down the Hierarchy of Needs. This is why I maintain that, by its nature, paring options is a dark art. It is also the single most powerful skill a person can learn in influencing human behavior. Do not use this casually. Misapplied, the outcomes can be disastrous for you and your target.

Matrix of Fulfillment (How to Satisfy Maslow)

Maslow's Hierarchy starts with basic needs such as food, water, shelter, sleep, and sex, with the animal needs on a very broad tier. The visual representation of it as the base of a pyramid makes sense, because it is the foundation of all the other tiers of needs. The items you need to meet these basic animal needs are relatively easy to find, but when you cannot find them, you cannot move to the next tier. In a congested, famine-stricken area one finds it hard to maintain his esteem while fighting for an apple. As you move up the pyramid, it gets harder and harder to ascend to the next tier, as opportunities to find a new group diminish, or it takes significant effort to gain or regain self-esteem.

Ironically, though the opportunities become more rare as you move up the pyramid, the number of actions that could fulfill each of these needs actually broadens. When you are thirsty, hungry, or need shelter or sleep, the options are narrow. When you are at the point of self-actualization, however, the options are endless. So while all the money in the world will not keep you from dying of thirst while stranded on a raft in the ocean, maybe you can be self-actualized through having the world's most extensive collection of shoehorns used by Elvis.

So if you overlaid a diagram of the Hierarchy of Fulfillment over the pyramid of Maslow's Hierarchy of Needs, the result would look like this:

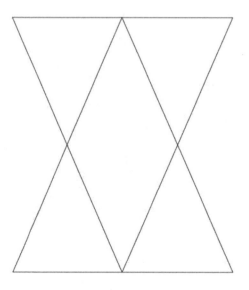

As the diagram indicates, the possibilities for fulfillment of the higher needs get broader and broader, so that only the physiological ones are tightly constricted. We walk though life inherently aware that, aside from those animal needs, anything is possible (or so our self-help gurus would have us believe). But there is yet another critical factor: situation.

Situation

You come home and your spouse asks you what you would like to eat. You say you would like lemongrass chicken. Unfortunately, you live in a small town in Kansas where there is no lemongrass at the supermarket and no Thai restaurant within 85 miles. In this case, you failed to understand the situation, to assess what the possibilities are. So, the situation itself pares the options.

Would you ever drink water with rat feces in it? Of course not. That's insane. How about cow feces? At this point, you think I've lost my train of thought even asking that question. But what if your only source of water was either a well suffering from a rat infestation or a muddy pond where cows hung out? That is precisely the choice that Maryann faced in the first Eco-Challenge, a race encompassing more than 376 miles of spectacular Utah wilderness, much of which also happened to be very, very dry. Racers who made it as far as the well and the pond—many did not—all faced the same options: (1) use some fabric as a filter as you pour the contaminated water into a bottle and add iodine or (2) go into a state of dehydration and get kicked out of the race. About 100 people chose to drink the water. Maryann would normally not have considered that an option, but the situation forced the issue. In this case, she was still functioning at a high enough level for the dynamics of both triangles to meet. She opted to forgo esteem and drink dung water rather than walk away from the race and further shatter her esteem.

In a very real-life situation, in which there were no camera crews or other people around, all would have opted for the same decision, not for esteem reasons, but for the most basic reason of thirst.

This diagram shows the real imperative—the real choice of options in the diagram.

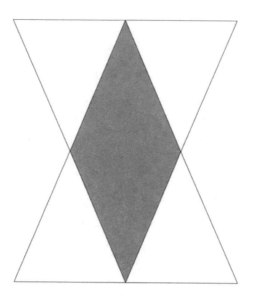

So no matter what the magical mystery self-help books say, for real human beings, the true options are limited. The shaded diamond delineates the area of actual options and it reflects these premises:

⇨   Few people have the ability to move their reality to the point that their self-actualization tier (the peak of Maslow's pyramid) can touch all of the possible options. Why? Your operating system and the output of what's running on it (experiences) limit your capability to maneuver through the tiers, so as you move up the tiers, the options become slimmer. The resulting possible options you have are based on situation and prior decisions.

⇨   The broadest range of possibilities for most of us exist in the tier of belonging and love. Does that really surprise you when you think about how many people never truly get to the point of real self-esteem?

How you perceive yourself in terms of possibilities also narrows your options. Look at your own core personality and the 3-D bell that represents your strengths and weaknesses, your ordinariness and your differentiation. There are only so many things that will allow you to get to the point of self-actualization. The universe of possibilities is large, but not for an individual with a limited number of talents and interests, which is really any of us.

So on a theoretical level, there are infinite ways for humans to become self-actualized, but on a practical level, they narrow. If we carried no baggage from the past, any given thing could satisfy that need, but every decision limits the next, and before you know it, the options are narrow. Once you acknowledge this, you negate the presumption that people have unlimited ways to feel truly satisfied. As you go toward the base of Maslow's Hierarchy, there are fewer ways to satisfy the needs on each level. As you keep dropping down, the more primate the need, the fewer the natural options. So the broadest range of options lies in the place where the monkey and the man meet: belonging and esteem.

Your knowledge of this reality combined with your situational awareness and analysis of an individual enable you to get people to do things they cannot imagine. That level of control starts with putting yourself in the right circumstance. Regardless of what it takes to satisfy someone's needs, if you have control of the circumstances, you can manage a person's perception of what the possibilities are.

The Landrum Factor

In codifying the process of paring options, I chose to name the system after Don Landrum, the most efficient practitioner of paring options I have ever met.

I worked with Don when I was in my 20s, so I've had a number of years to practice and integrate the operational principles I saw him use. In a nutshell, his art was the ability to make people see life as mundane and limited, even when it's not.

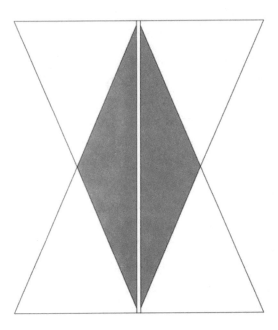

The diagram above illustrates that at the heart of all the possibilities to fulfill your needs and inside the narrowed options based on situation is a very narrow band of real—not imagined—possibilities. This band of possibilities is much narrower than the original for one simple reason: self-image.

Through manipulation, skilled interrogators can easily convince sources that, in areas where they think they are typical, they fall woefully short of the mark. And in areas of pride, they are just typical. How do we do it—how will you manage this?

⇨ Isolation.

⇨ Illustration.

⇨ Association.

Isolation

You do not have to lock your target in a cage. Merely separating the person from the support group that props up his self-image will accomplish isolation. For example, you accompany the local office goliath—highest equipment sales in the county—to a national sales conference. While others may know his name, it is by no means a household word. If he starts to raise his head in a way that undermines your agenda, you can quickly strike him down because his power base and self-image insulators are not around him in this setting. A natural way to do it might be spotlighting how small the county is.

You can also make isolation a contrived and pre-meditated exercise. You might choose to set up a meeting at his favorite restaurant, and at the last minute, change the setting to a restaurant where everyone knows your name just to set him off balance and undercut his self-image. The most powerful effect is to remove any source of self-image reinforcement.

Illustration

Through illustration, you ask him enough questions to dispel the notion that he has control of the topic at hand and unlimited options in a given situation. Once a person starts to see where his shortcomings are, it limits options he perceives as available. In using illustration, you will use your questioning and listening skills to pinpoint things he does not want to come out and feelings of inadequacy related to meeting core requirements of the group. Once identified, you prey on them by questioning with intent.

Association

The art of associating plays on the idea that each choice eliminates another. By showing association with one group, you eliminate the ability to bond with another. The result is that you narrow a person's options even further than the situation dictated.

Another insidious form of association relies on your use of the 3-D bell on the alpha of that group. You determine where he is inadequate and highlight it. Because that alpha enjoys super-typical status in your target's world, how great can the group be? The person's association with the group led by this tainted alpha suddenly plays as a negative.

— — — — — —

In paring someone's options, you send the message that he can either follow a path to fulfillment that you've laid out, or do what he wants with unknown consequences. You narrow the choices so that the only way he can belong or continue to differentiate is to do what you want, to take the path you've chosen for him. That path has appeal, because you connect it with the promise of meeting whatever his pressing need is in the Hierarchy.

In the interrogation world, this is simple. The two parties are enemies, and the one is dependent on the other. Based on the chain of events that led to the situation, the options for the prisoner are very limited to begin with. The interrogator may take the road of trickery, asking the prisoner to give him something of dubious value and then making the prisoner feel like what he gave was a great deal of information. The interrogator then uses this as a lever to say to the prisoner, "I'm going tell the entire prison population that you just helped the enemy, unless…." The message is clear: the interrogator will differentiate this prisoner from the rest of his group in a negative fashion to make him an outcast.

Fearing loss of camaraderie, the prisoner asks the interrogator not to disclose the information. Always willing to "help," the interrogator tells the prisoner he would have no need to divulge anything to the others if the prisoner would just help him complete the details. The prisoner is faced with a dilemma: Give up more details and save face with fellow prisoners, or remain principled and not say anything else. Choosing sacred principles means he not only will lose reputation for having talked in the first place but, more importantly, he will also lose the belonging of his fellow countrymen. The allure of violating just one more time to save that bond wins out.

Take it to even greater extremes. A person who has walked into a situation feeling self-assured, but has his ego battered, his comrades isolated from him, and his physical well-being threatened, has sunk all the way down to the bottom—the level of physiological needs. The interrogator has pared his options to the point where he will do what's asked of him for a cookie.

In the History Channel's *We Can Make You Talk*, my colleagues and I faced volunteers with various backgrounds, but all came in with a confidence that they would do well in the two-day simulation. One young man in particular hung his superior attitude on his academic credentials; he came into this role-playing exercise asserting that he would show these cretins from the U.S. Army that he could put them to shame.

He was a 28-year-old, self-actualized college professor who found out his title and degrees meant nothing in that environment. All his snooty demeanor did was kick us into high gear with psychological techniques designed to break him. Those credentials were and are impressive, but we would never reinforce his self-image by saying that, and neither would his fellow prisoners, who had their own self-image to worry about. He was isolated from admirers.

This was a guy who walked into the simulation seeing himself as differentiated—intelligent, well educated, and well bred—but we set about paring him back to the point that all he had left was enough dignity to belong, and let him know that if he did one more thing that went against us, we would remove that dignity, and he would be left grasping for belonging.

When we interviewed him, we took every opportunity to point out to this tall, skinny guy that he was not physically gifted. That is an easy starting point with someone who is young. The rigors of movement and the physical nature of the reality-TV abduction took their toll on all of our participants. There were women in the group who held up much better than the professor—a point not wasted on us. I drove home the fact to the professor that a young woman sitting near him had fared much better than he had physically, and that we thought he couldn't even stand up to a little girl. His reaction was sad, comical, and predicable: "I have a brilliant mind." That became his tag for the rest of the exercise. When we would drag him from room to room blindfolded, and insult his manliness, we always used his nickname: Brilliant Mind.

We interrupted his charisma cycle as soon as we responded to his introduction. His credentials carried no meaning in our world—a fact we quickly demonstrated by illustration and isolation. Once we had him to the point of rolling over, he became our point of association for the others: Is this the best of your breed? Was he brilliant? Absolutely. In the way a computer programmer is brilliant in the jungles of Borneo. Pure knowledge, no application.

We took a quick look at his 3-D bell and found the areas where he felt inadequate. Then we overlaid these onto his strengths. Each time we identified a strength, we mocked it, wearing him down to where he questioned whether even that strength was real. What we used against him were human interpersonal skills that preyed on his own feelings and fears of inadequacy.

In undermining his confidence, we also demonstrated to him that he wasn't what he thought he was. As his confidence eroded, he even questioned whether or not he belonged in his peer group. Brilliant Mind gave himself an F and sunk lower in Maslow's Hierarchy.

Ultimately, we sent in a threat—a big, fierce-looking interrogator he perceived as stupid and dangerous. The professor responded to one of our own by offering to trade information for insulation—and a cookie.

Paring Options: How You Do It

The SERE school and interrogation simulations for television capture extreme circumstances, in which a subject may well plunge all the way down to the bottom level of the Hierarchy. If anything like that happens in your workplace, then you probably have a job in a maximum-security penitentiary.

Your first step is to plot the bell curve for the person you want to influence. Is this person a self-actualized, super-typical person such as the young college professor in the simulation I described, or is he struggling to meet needs lower in the Hierarchy?

You take someone from a self-actualized place by doing exactly what we did with the college professor: you don't acknowledge that his differentiator demonstrates any value. Instead of Oprah Winfrey the media mogul, you talk to Oprah the poor child from Mississippi. You make the person feel as though she has to show you she's more. You manage the person's state.

Clingers—those who are uncertain of their place in a group—are fair game, open to attack because they are barely hanging onto their status within the group. I know a woman with an accent that can best be described as idiosyncratic European; she has never even been outside of the United States, nor does she have a family that speaks oddly. Her accent is a source of fascination for some of her colleagues, however, who find it amusing that this pretty, smart woman has come up with a twisted tongue that's all her own. Most people in the group feel more marginal about it, however, and when one of the relatively unpopular (translate: sub-typical) people in the group called her on it, it was like he'd taken his boot to her head and kicked her down the social ladder. All eyes were on her.

In a moment, among the people who were present, her eccentricity overtook her amusing cuteness. He bounced her down to his sub-typical level. By attacking her position in the group, and forcing her to make sudden moves to normalize in order to keep her place in the social structure, he effectively did two things: He took away her differentiator and forced her to fear for her sense of belonging. That split second of personal doubt is the upper hand in interpersonal relations. In this situation, he had little to lose, and she little to gain.

Most of this book relies on skills that you can use to raise or lower someone in Maslow's Hierarchy. The best solution is one that causes a person to rise, because you will be viewed as charismatic and good. If you use this skill set associated with paring options, your aim is moving people down the Hierarchy. Few people—at least not the ones with any self-respect—will respond to you kindly. Consider your own reputation and your need to belong. This is not child's play.

Take Him Down

It's much easier to pare options as you move people down the levels of the Hierarchy than up. The only options they have left are the ones that will serve the needs of the level they are on. If they don't do what you want them to do, they limit options for growth, or worse yet, you push them down farther, and their options become even narrower.

By relying on the 3-D model of your target to visualize the whole person relative to his world, you will see where his areas of pride are. Understand these areas of pride may have nothing to do with belonging to the group against which you are trying to manipulate him. Even if you are levering him against the people at work, and his greatest strength is not at work, you may not see the correlation, but the correlation is there as a lever.

Here's how it works. He will be very proud of his grandest accomplishment, so you can use this pride and the tools of illustration to differentiate him in a way that separates him from the norm for the group. By separate, I do not mean make him feel superior or gain friends—just the opposite. You want to spotlight his special talent with color that makes it seem elitist or wacky: "How'd that dingy race to Tangiers Island go last month, Earl?" To which he replies that it was a yacht race, and can't help but come across as snooty.

Self-image drives all of this, so what seems perfectly normal to him for the outside group where he's insulated may seem bizarre when you start to illustrate exactly what it means. For example, I do a sport that involves people wearing armor and beating the heck out of each other with sticks. Working in the business world with golfers as I do, it takes a certain personality type to be able to withstand scrutiny of my hobby. Well insulated in the world where the sport is normal, what I do raises no eyebrows. Standing in a group of people who have no idea what the details are, and repeatedly ask questions about the intricacies of the hobby, could take a person who lacks confidence off center. The easiest way to know you have an "in" to influence someone like this is when you find a person who is highly differentiated outside the group with which you are dealing, but few in that group know about that differentiation.

Once you start to separate your target from the group, the next step is to offer him an out that ties him back to the group and is bonded to your success. You might call for a consensus on a decision that had been going against you, and with his vote, you win. Or it may mean that he takes on some extra work to make your life easier.

The pattern is this:

⇨   Fracture him from the group with knowledge you have gained in modeling.

⇨   Illustrate the point, or just openly divulge it.

⇨   Once the fracture is evident, give him a clear option to do something that you want, which will allow him to rebound, avert further loss of face, or allow him to continue down the path of his choosing and lose even more ground with the group.

This is one of the most powerful forms of a threat-and-rescue technique. When you are done, the target will never forget it, although he may not understand how you accomplished what you did.

Paring options is a style of getting what you want that leaves a mark. With time and mastery, you can get to the point of subtlety, but in the beginning most people have a tendency to be harsh with this skill set. The person who has been manipulated this way will likely not forget it. Just like any other choice you make, this one will change the options you have later. As an interrogator I may never see the person again. I can afford to be casual with the relationship. Daily life doesn't make it that easy to get away.

I am giving you knowledge of this core art of interrogation because there are some people who invite this treatment with their own "art." When I see someone who prides himself on being a manipulator, and who tries his tricks on me, I retaliate with this. Most of the time, he slinks off, having lost face, and I never have to deal with the issue again.

As I discuss in the following chapters, there are other, much more subtle and kind ways to get cooperation.

CHAPTER 8

Strategies to Move Your Human

A brief recap: Knowing what drives a person will give you the foundation information for getting what you want. Your first task is finding out where he is in terms of belonging and differentiating; that is, where he fits in the Hierarchy. You have the tools to understand what the possibilities are for him moving up in the Hierarchy—in most cases better than he can.

Your range of options take shape as you decide whether to help him differentiate in the group, perhaps raising him to super-typical status, or downgrade him to plain old Joe. From the moment you make that decision, your entire plan to get what you want reflects whether you will move him up or move him down. By up or down, I do not mean only between tiers, but also within a tier. Your target who is barely belonging has a need to firm up his position. Will you take the approach that threatens to remove him from the group entirely unless he cooperates, move him squarely into the group in exchange for his cooperation, or a combination of the two? Your target, who is fully differentiated to the point of being super-typical, has risen above the tier for belonging, and may be climbing the stairs to self-actualization. Do you take the approach that differentiates him even further—the kick-him-upstairs move—or reduce his differentiators by pointing out that the emperor's new clothes are really just skin?

At this juncture, I can't tell you what you are likely to choose, because every situation will be dependent on what you know about your target—how he views himself and the world, his strengths and weaknesses, as well as where you are in the group. What I can tell you is how each tool works in the context of the different strategies:

⇨ Bonding.

⇨ Fracturing.

⇨ Homogenizing.

⇨ Overdifferentiating.

At the same time, I can show you how each of these works in concert with paring options, isolation, illustration, and association.

Bonding and Homogenizing

Bonding is the positive use of finding commonalities among people. It points to the things you have in common, good or bad, and invites someone to come closer by suggesting, "You and I are so much alike that I can't be a threat to you." Even clichés such as "misery loves company," and "strength in numbers" capture this gravitation toward those with whom we share some feeling, trait, or cause.

Homogenizing is a negative use of finding the commonalities among people; that is, the negative use of bonding. The preacher is no different from the congregation: He has the same human drives and frailties as the rest of the congregation. This can be the preacher caught philandering or the boss making mistakes in a presentation. Whatever the genesis, the outcome is the same. By deliberately homogenizing, you push the target back closer to the center of the group, and away from super-typical status. Through the use of the tactics I described in the section on paring options, you can apply the following strategies.

Illustration

How effectively you illustrate what you know about the target has a tremendous effect on the quality of outcome, whether the intent is to bond or to homogenize. You can carry out the strategy by asking straightforward questions, forcing a behavior, or by parallel questioning to draw the person to divulge information publicly and unintentionally.

Bonding Through Illustration

Illustration relies on the tactics you learned in Chapter 4. Whether you opt to use direct questioning or parallel questioning to get your target to divulge information is dependent on what you know about his personality from modeling him. Once you decide, you then go about questioning or bringing up topics in an obtuse way that you know he will comment on.

In some cases all you need to do is issue the invitation, and he will do the rest. You are, after all, creating an opportunity for him to bond—one of the most powerful of human drives.

Larry King does a great job of humanizing people for several reasons; for example, he points to ways in which they have commonalities with other people. Many interviewers focus on what makes the celebrity guest special or unique, whereas King has a talent for illustrating the link between the celebrity and the audience. With a few simple very human questions, he can find out how Jennifer Aniston feels about a public relationship ending in divorce. By doing that, he takes away all of her money, fashions, and fame. He is talking to the person, not the star. When he finishes the conversation, the star has gained connection and power with the audience, because you see that, for all of her super-typical status, she is still human.

Homogenizing Through Illustration

Use homogenizing to take away your target's special powers, such as Lex Luthor uses kryptonite to turn Superman into a regular man. As I said, when someone is super-typical in one area, he is going to be equally sub-typical in another. A quick review of the pantheon of Greek gods shows petty, vain, and conniving gods with supernatural powers. Does it surprise you that humans would invent gods that represent this aspect of human nature?

In its simplest form, homogenizing is pointing out the everyday human frailties of the god, such as being in your workplace or community. In its most insidious and complex form, it is causing the super-typical to disclose something that makes him mundane or even sub-typical. The range of possibilities is endless. Humans love to see shooting stars fall back to earth. Turn on the entertainment news; there is a version of the Britney Spears burnout every day.

Britney Spears is a prime example of creating an arena for the spectacle of destruction. Build it and they will come. Often, the easiest way to get a super-typical to divulge information that proves he is not so super is to start a conversation in which he thinks you admire him, and then work your way into the details. If you tell him he is grand, and he's the pretentious type, for example, he will gladly tell you how grand. As you question what he does on Saturdays and he tells you about his singing gig, you ask about how his wife takes that, and he tells you he is recently divorced—a fact he was concealing from his coworkers. You may be able to stop right there.

On a more positive note, through illustration of the super-powers of the rest of the group, you can also cause the super-typical to feel rather average. The effect is he loses a bit of his bravado, which in turn makes the rest of the group bond more closely to him and homogenize him.

Whether used to bond or homogenize, illustration is a great tool, because you are using the person's own words and deeds to establish commonality. No words of yours can ever have the power that the words and action of the target do.

Isolation

In the discussion of the interrogation cycle, I noted that most soldiers are not held captive with their entire unit, because the nature of war fragments the group. In an interrogation, the source is removed from his insulating group; therefore, he is physically separated from the folks who give him his sense of self-image. The result is that all self-image inputs come from the interrogators. I have used manipulation of self-image harshly when pointing out a superficial scratch as "looking bad" over and over. The prisoner became so obsessed by it that he paid little attention to anything else.

For you, the equivalent use of isolation doesn't necessarily involve physical separation, but as I previously described, it does mean taking away the positive reinforcement of self-image.

Bonding Through Isolation

By reforming a group into subsets, you can easily skew the norm of the larger group. You've seen a version of this occur naturally many times as a group goes from focusing on a single topic of conversation to splintering into multiple conversations. Some people will suddenly start showing off their knowledge of the subject, and others will suddenly be left out. Let's say you instigate this in a department meeting by breaking the group into special teams. You can give the subset a new member who has not yet established his belonging in the department, and set the task for the subset to his strengths. He thereby gets a chance to create real value and belonging; and when he returns to the larger group, the snowball effect will give him leverage to feel as though he belongs. It may even allow him to begin to differentiate. This happens all of the time in corporate America when sub-teams are created arbitrarily and someone rises to the occasion. The difference here is that you use the tool of isolation to create an incubator for the personality of the person with whom you are trying to bond.

Homogenizing Through Isolation

In much the same way the new guy found belonging, you can create specialty teams of a group where the super-typical's magic holds little sway. You could isolate him to the big pond where the barracuda live, for example: "I've asked that you give the department's presentation at the board meeting, Ralph." When he returns from the ocean to the gold fish pond a couple of pints of blood low, he might feel more like teaming with the people there. His big realization may be that he is really not such a big fish after all, or it may be that he suddenly realizes other people in his little pond have talents, too. Either way, you inflicted heavy doses of reality on his self-image. You are, in effect, applying the Landrum Factor through action.

Association

With Maslow's Hierarchy and the matrix of satisfaction in the forefront of your mind, you're going to make some practical use out of your knowledge of why and how options to fulfill needs can be limited. First of all, every choice you make limits later choices. So if you get baptized Mormon, your chances of becoming the Roman Catholic Pope go away. Every association you make, whether with a group, a belief, or an action limits possibilities for your future. Although the tools of illustration play into how you apply your knowledge of someone's affiliations or connections, the use of association as a strategy will cause the group to see the outsider as more like them, and accept him. Or it will do the opposite: they will see that the silk purse is just a sow's ear.

Bonding Through Association

Through your knowledge of the person, you can find common ground for the barely belonging. In some cases, it is nothing more than the fact that he knows someone they know. In others, it may be association with like people or social groups. Jack and Susan are both parents of 6th graders; they share similar experiences thanks to developmental psychology. If both have suffered through implementation of some major initiative at work, they have common ground. It does not matter how miniscule the commonality of association. What matters is how similar it is. Two women who are deacons of separate church denominations will share more than two people who've been to Graceland. The key is to associate your target with something that has meaning to the others in the group. I saw this happen dramatically at a recent meeting when someone volunteered that she wore a pink wristband because she was a breast cancer survivor. Everyone at the table—men and women—at least knew someone very well who was also a breast cancer survivor.

People also commonly engender bonding through association by joining professional groups in which members have shared goals and skills. Based on what you know about your target, you can bring out something much more interesting and obscure that has meaning in the setting.

Homogenizing Through Association

When you know about an association that reduces the elevated status of the super-typical, you point that out to homogenize. A prime example of this plays out on the daily news as we see the families of the rich and famous show up again and again with ordinary problems. Lindsay Lohan's father ends up in jail. Cher's daughter gains a lot of weight. It is tough to appear to be better than everyone else when you are associated with regular folks with run-of-the-mill problems.

In an example much closer to home, you may know that your target, John, has hung around someone well known as a philanderer. You ask if he's seen the guy recently. He responds that he saw him right after he got back from his vacation in Cancun. With eyebrows up in a look between surprise and shock, you say, "Oh yeah? I heard that Cancun trip caused his divorce." No matter how super-typical John is, his soft, white underbelly has just been exposed.

— — — — —

Just as in establishing charisma, too much bonding and showing similarities to other people takes away the magic of the super-typical. By walking the knife's edge, you can gain the respect and authority of those around you. People of high esteem and reputation are walking on a different knife; that edge marks the difference between being human and being more than human.

Envision belonging as a radial, just as you envisioned personality types in a radial diagram. Positive outcomes occupy one side, and negative the other. You move your target around through isolation, illustration, and association to shift him from barely belonging to a solid member of the group, to supertypical status and all the way down to monkey.

Fracturing to Differentiate or Overdifferentiate

Fracturing is about showing difference. Not a negative or a positive difference, just difference. How you use each of the tools will determine how the differences are perceived.

Fracturing to Differentiate

This is a positive application of differences—pointing out areas where a member of the group has strengths that allow him to rise like cream. This application relies on bringing strengths to the fore—things that cannot possibly alienate others, or at least that's the plan.

Fracturing to Overdifferentiate

By "overdifferentiate," I mean going so far in any direction that others in the group cannot identify with the person, or that he can no longer sanely identify with the group. This does not necessarily mean the differentiator is negative. Maybe it's something simple, such as his getting an invitation to the boss's country club because he went to college with the boss's daughter. That alone could make him so distinctive in the group he is in that the group can no longer fulfill his need. Clichés in English such as "you can never go home again" have their roots in this principle.

Fracturing Through Illustration

To sell a product, you have to know why it isn't like other products, even if it's just cheaper. Using the tools you learned in Chapter 4, you need to draw out little-known facts about your target to find out what makes him different. Whether by asking difficult questions only someone with his skill set could answer, or using approaches to provoke an outburst in a meeting, masterful use of the tools is requisite to applying this strategy.

Differentiating Through Illustration

When you ask questions, tailor the questions in such a way that they make him appear to be solidly one of the group with insights the other members of the group do not have. (Leading questions can help here.) Whether the information involves a past job, hobby, or other extracurricular activity, create a spider web of links from him to the skill set. Use thought-provoking parallel questions to get him to the point that he sees the correlation and brings it out, or simply ask him what he would have done in his past job. The skill set is about allowing him to be the hero, and show how he is super-typical in some way without taking it to the point of golden-haired child or brownnoser.

Overdifferentiating Through Illustration

In our modern world of anything goes and "there is no right or wrong," people can easily forget the fact that something can be just too different. Regardless of what they spout in public, many people are much more conservative than they let on. I do not mean politically, but rather that they tolerate few deviations from the norm than they care to admit out of political correctness.

Asking questions that push a topic to the edge provokes both revealing answers and behaviors. Craft questions and approaches to lever someone to a point of overreacting or sloughing off something important to the group as "nothing more than nonsense." One example is using a leading question to imply judgment: "Don't you think that parachuting off that bridge while kids were walking home from school constitutes reckless endangerment?" The effect is to separate him from what is acceptable for the group.

This strategy works especially well when someone who is well-respected has an opinion not based in fact, or claims some guru's thoughts as his own: "If the geodesic dome is such an energy-efficient model, why don't we see more of them now that we're painfully aware of the cost of energy?" You offer him the opportunity to explain, stroking him if he sounds intelligent—to a point—and then switch to critical questioning. Then, you can chose to rescue him or let him founder.

Either way, your work is done, and he will either need to establish himself as a member of the group or find belonging elsewhere. I saw this in action recently with someone who presented himself as a network marketing genius, but finally had to admit that his financial history felt like a rollercoaster ride.

Differentiating Through Isolation

It is often difficult to have someone seem special in a hostile pool or one populated by uniquely talented fish. In some cases, a super-typical has used precisely the same talent that an average guy in the room possesses to rise to the level of super-typical. Unless the super-typical is well balanced, she may see the new guy as a threat and intimidate him. His rescue is having the ability to enter a smaller pool where he can comfortably belong. If you make that happen, you create a buffer between the new guy and the paranoid super-typical. Ways to do this can be a contrived meeting change that inadvertently removes the super-typical from the environment, or an invitation to the new guy to participate in something of which the threatened super-typical would never be. Both of these isolate your target to allow her to shine.

Overdifferentiating Through Isolation

Some things that are perfectly acceptable in some groups are just too much in others. If I used the same language in corporate America that I used in the military, I would be run out of the building. By adeptly maneuvering your target to feel as though he is safe and among friends, you can often get your target to disclose facts that he would not in armed camps. This works well in life and in comedy. Both rely on the fact that humans are creatures of ritual, repeating the same things over and over involuntarily. In the comedy *Guess Who*, Ashton Kutcher, who is dating Bernie Mac's daughter, is at her house for Thanksgiving dinner. Intensely disliking the fact that this white boy is dating his daughter, Bernie Mac baits him into telling "black jokes," luring him with the message, "Come on you're family now." Eventually, Kutcher falls into repeating joke after joke until he crosses the line.

This phenomenon of turning on the tap happens all the time when people project that acceptance means that someone is exactly like them, and will accept them, warts and all. That's rarely true.

Differentiating Through Association

People differentiate through association all the time by name-dropping or telling you where they went to school. A friend of mine from New Jersey often says that living in Princeton makes people feel smart; you get credentials by saying, "I'm from Princeton." Manipulating associations can make someone appear to have more or less value to the group. When he is a solid member of the team, and knows the boss's brother well, that might be enough to raise him up—unless the boss's brother is similar to former President Jimmy Carter's brother, Billy, a self-proclaimed alcoholic. Every association the person has, whether voluntary or accidental, can make a tremendous difference. Look at people such as Anderson Cooper.

He is competent in his own right, but how much help did he get from being Gloria Vanderbilt's son?

Overdifferentiating Through Association

This has been done to drive guilt or innocence in courts all over the United States. If you hang out with unsavory characters, what does that make you? You could be Charles Manson or you could be Mother Teresa. The key here is how the spin is handled. By associating your target with someone who is outside the realm of understanding the group, you move the person to a point of isolation, and maybe closer to bonding with you or another group.

In a very public way, this has occurred to Jim Bakker, Jimmy Swaggart, and even United States presidents. Association with unsavory individuals or concepts leaves a person grasping to belong. As he tries to belong, he forgets all about being super-typical and tries his best to hold on. In the case of the self-actualized, he tries to maintain his reputation similar to President Clinton. In the case of Swaggart and his prostitutes, or Bakker and his ministry's payoff to Jessica Hahn, the damage is so intense, they beg forgiveness and remind the congregation they're human in an attempt to hold on. Some rise again. Not usually, though.

Whatever your strategy, make it a success from the start by building that 3-D model of your target. Keep refining your understanding of his need in terms of the Hierarchy, where he fits in his group, how you can characterize his self-image, and what his sources are of pride and shame. You can only get the desired results if you base your plan on data. Ideally, you will create a map for his success that leads down the road to yours.

CHAPTER 9

The Final Factor

Where is your target on the Hierarchy of Needs, and what do you do with the answer?

Given that you now have a background in skills and methods that interrogators use to influence behavior, I'll pull them together in a program summary for closing the deal with your target—for getting what you want. Part of that program is something I've covered only tangentially throughout the book: self-reflection. Where are you on the Hierarchy of Needs and what are your options for fulfillment?

Action Plan

The outline of your actions is straightforward: look at where the person is in his life in terms of needs, and tie his success in achieving those needs to your outcome. In terms of mechanics, you look at the person holistically and figure out ways to raise or lower them in the Hierarchy. In some cases, they will not even know where they sit and what they need. You will help them by showing them what the possibilities are, and then paring and shaping the options to realize those possibilities.

Center your process on the intersection of Maslow's Hierarchy and the matrix of fulfillment. Most people sit on or between the tiers of belonging and differentiating, or the need for love and connection and the need for status and reputation. Your 3-D model of the person gives you a holistic view of where he fits in his various groups. Your interaction with him through use of your tools tells you where he thinks he fits and what that means to him. Knowing his drives, needs, and current situation you can see—most likely much better than your target—what options fall within that diamond that constitutes the intersection of the Hierarchy and the matrix. Your power lies in not only identifying those options, but having a plan to use them to move your target up or down: to strengthen his belonging or weaken it, to raise his status or lower it, to assist him toward self-actualization or damage chances of achieving it.

And that, in a nutshell, is how you get him to do what you want. When you know what he needs, you align his arrows to your arrows. When you know what he desires, which may not match what he needs, you change his wants because *the need overrides the want.* If a person aims for self-actualization through a promotion at work, and you push him into a position of need, such as needing to regain status because you effectively homogenized him, then you can force him to adjust his focus. You can then attack the need instead of the want.

This is precisely what I did in the interrogation in which I wanted my source to divulge more than the name of his commander. He wanted to maintain his loyalty through silence, which is an attempt to maintain self-esteem, so I threatened to spotlight him as an example to other prisoners of someone who cooperated with the enemy—unless he actually did give me the information I sought. As his need to belong to his group seized his focus, he abandoned his desire to take the high road. I forced him to choose between self-esteem and belonging, and the lower the need on the pyramid, the higher the likelihood it is going to win out.

Once you know how to align his need to your want, you have a good chance that you will get what you want. You just need to establish and reinforce that you are the light, the way, and the gate, and that's why you need the interrogator methods of discovery, techniques of manipulation, and strategies and tactics of bonding and fracturing. Pull out these tools from your toolbox to do one of four things to close the deal:

⇨ You show what you can do for him, do it, and expect something in return.

⇨ You show what you can do for him, do it, and threaten to take it away unless you get what you want.

⇨   You show what you can do to get in his way, but offer not to if he does what you want.

⇨   You show what you can do to get in his way, do it, and only offer to rescue him if he does what you want.

This process could take minutes, hours, weeks, or decades, depending on the scope of what you want, the time you have to get to know the person, and your proficiency with the skill sets I've described.

In the world of interrogation, we work quickly because we have to. If all you want is a piece of information, then you might work just as quickly by assessing where the person is on the Hierarchy, giving him feedback that presents your ability to meet a need, and then asking for the information. The scenario: You see someone working a bar with no customers. She's bored and lonely, signaling an immediate need to belong. You sit down and talk, asking questions about customers who usually come in to find out if your spouse might be one of them.

What if you have a grander desire, say president of your company. What you want is the backing of the board of directors. Big scope. Same process. Could take awhile.

Making Maslow Personal

In Maslow's Hierarchy of Needs, you can only climb up to the next tier once you have met the needs of the tier you're on. Analogously, every decision you make about how to fulfill those needs affects your options for further fulfillment.

I've made the point over and over that you, as the person outside looking in at your target, may well see that person's needs far better than he does. You are also in a position to access objectively whether he is now, or can readily become, super-typical, typical, or sub-typical in his group—regardless of where he thinks he is. Try to use your modeling and analysis skills on yourself, too, in an effort to give yourself perspective on personality, sources of pride and shame, strengths, and weaknesses. You might be very surprised, and even realize why what you want someone to do is completely off base—that what you want does not match what you really *need.*

When I was a much younger man (in my 20s), I shared a house with two other people; both were Special Forces operators; that is, specially trained, highly regarded, super-typical soldiers. One of my best friends from high school, who was also a soldier, dropped by to visit, and mentioned how I did not seem like the old me. I was more subdued. What he picked up was how I felt in that house—not subdued, but clearly not the alpha I had been among my friends at home. In the following weeks, my two roommates had the opportunity to see me interrogate. After watching me get into someone's head, my roommates had a newfound respect for me, and equal amounts of deference. Although I could have lived without it, I admit I was very happy to have their deference. I was now differentiated, not only among my kind, but also among some of the most alpha in the military.

That experience told me something important about myself. Although I was clearly differentiated among my group of interrogators, I still lacked confidence with my roommates, whom I considered friends. Discovering something like this about yourself will keep you tuned into the fact that many of the people you profile will have similar gaps in self-awareness as it pertains to belonging and differentiating. Feeling differentiated in an environment outside of work gives some people a false sense of fitting higher in the pecking order at work than they actually do. Conversely, they might think that differentiation doesn't do anything for their status in the group, but as I've shown you, it very well might.

Distilling the Process

As I cover each of the following types, I focus on how the person actually fits into the group, and not a perspective warped by gaps in self-awareness. I'll distill that down even more: it's how the person fits in terms of something you can change. Some things are beyond your ability to change, so although you know she fits as a sub-typical in her family, you cannot fix that to get what you want. Maybe you can, however, help her to belong in the work environment, and eventually become super-typical there. So while you know about lots of other places where your target operates, the one we are talking about here is the one over which you have control.

An Outsider Desperate to Belong

No man is an island. If you find someone who is an outsider looking in, searching for a way to open the door, you have but one option: a positive one. You can help him demonstrate value to the group as the basis for a bond, or use the snowball effect of having one person and then another accept him until the group welcomes him. Any method to help him will make him feel indebted. Use the tools you know to find his strengths and value, and then illustrate, isolate, and associate until the group cannot miss the reasons for bringing this person in. Knowing the route to bringing him in, you can always throw the process in reverse to fracture him back out if necessary.

Belongs Comfortably

Right after someone feels accepted, he gets comfortable, and has not yet found that simply being a member is not fulfilling. At this point, belonging in and of itself can become a differentiator from those who do not belong. You have two options with someone at this stage: show him you can fracture him from the group, thus creating anxiety, or show him there is so much more than what he has experienced. This happens many times when a young initiate full of talent is seen by the group as a find, but has no idea of his own talent. He is in awe, thinking he has found a group that will complete him, or at least who are his equals. Once he gets comfortably inside, he starts to feel as though the members of the group are just like everyone else. When you spot someone at this stage, help him to understand the group is really not fit to be his peers, and that he could easily move past them. Sound familiar? That's how Anakin got to be Darth Vader. It is an archetypal story of impatience tempted by destructive forces that plays out every day. You have the tools to lure the young apprentice to your side, or to prevent it.

Fully Belongs, Middle-of-the-road, and Working to Differentiate

Getting comfortable in the organization can take a while or be immediate. Personality type can be a big factor here in that a person might walk into an environment seeing the trappings of similar types. As soon as he is certain of belonging, the need to show his unique stuff begins. Regardless of whether it is minor moves to differentiate or grand posturing, he begins to show he is more than a simple recruit. At this point the options become a little more complex: Do you homogenize his attempts to differentiate using isolation, illustration, and association? Or do you turn the tools to his favor and help him to stand out? Either way, you decide whether he is allowed to continue to differentiate or whether you put the brakes on his progress.

I could go on and on with types at various stages of belonging and differentiating, but these templates for action should give you enough framework so that you can create action plans for all of them.

Cashing In

In getting exactly what you want, you don't want to sound like a thug on a street: "Gimme your cash or I'll shoot your dog." You will set up the program so that your target's need is tied to your want. If you are manipulating someone within your group at work, then his need should not be a place in the church choir, and your want should not be his girlfriend.

EXERCISE: TAILORING FOR
REAL PEOPLE

Select two very different people in your organization whom you have no intention of targeting to get what you want. Place each one in one of these categories:

⇨   *An outsider desperate to belong.*

⇨   *Belongs comfortably.*

⇨   *Fully belongs, middle-of-the-road, and working to differentiate.*

⇨   *Fully belongs, differentiating on schedule.*

⇨   *Fully belongs, mostly differentiated; formal leader.*

⇨   *Fully belongs, mostly differentiated; natural leader.*

⇨   *Fully belongs, fully differentiated, approaching actualization.*

⇨   *Stagnant; one-sided belonging and differentiation; looking for more.*

Given that you can employ the strategies of bonding, homogenizing, differentiating, and overdifferentiating to maneuver a person through each of these categories, come up with a summary of your personalized action plan for how you would get what you want from them.

An example of how you can achieve clarity is in this story of a person we can categorize as earthy, who happens to be an outsider in her group.

⇨ *Who she is:* Martha wears skirts that are unfashionably long, low shoes, and wears her hair down with no style. When it's someone's birthday, she brings in cookies flecked with flax seeds. In the context of your downtown Washington, D.C., lobbying firm, you wonder how she ever got hired, even if it was as part of the backroom research staff. You've discovered that she has a passion for ballet and, in fact, danced professionally for four years. She likes to be at home with her cats.

⇨ *What you want:* You want to take the lead on shepherding a piece of potentially high-profile legislation through the Powers That Be on Capitol Hill, but you won't get the assignment unless you can prove you know more than one of the senior lobbyists. The only way to do that in the next two days—your window of opportunity—is if you get someone in research to work night and day for you without anyone else suspecting. So, no overtime.

⇨ *Basic question:* What is her need?

⇨ *Answer:* You discover she likes her job, just not her work environment. She *barely belongs* and has a hard time sitting in a cubicle every day next to people she considers materialistic, self-absorbed, and pretentious. She would like nothing more than to telecommute most of the time, but that will never happen unless someone over her boss decides that's appropriate. Ironically, if she could work at home, she would *belong comfortably*, which is her immediate need.

Options:

    o   Arrange to get her a flexible work schedule on a trial basis and expect payback.

    o   Show her you have the power to get her a flexible work schedule, but make getting what you want a condition of your action on her behalf.

    o   Arrange for someone to tell her that the best way to get a flexible work schedule is by pleasing you.

    o   Show her she will never get the privilege of telecommuting unless she does what you want.

The ideal, positive approach is to get what you want by raising her sense of belonging to a comfortable level. In this case, either of the positive options would serve that function, with the first one ceding some control to her, and the second keeping the control in your arena. Your modeling of her will give you the insights you need to know which approach she would respond better to.

Belonging and differentiating—that's what it comes down to. Similar to an interrogator, you now have the body of knowledge to make them happen. Maslow would have enjoyed you.

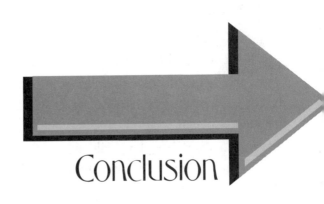

Conclusion

Human beings have lots of programs running all at once. Sometimes, despite the complexity, our behavior is predictable based on the premise of stimulus–response. Just like any other animal, we start at the bottom of the Hierarchy of Needs with food, shelter, and sex. We start to face myriad possibilities for fulfilling needs as we ascend to the higher, human levels where we seek self-esteem and self-actualization.

Does the pyramid of needs ever reach a point and end? I don't think so. As we continue to experience more and more, the point gets farther away, because more layers build up the pyramid. In other words, we don't reach the peak of self-actualization; we are always looking for something else. And at each level, we try to find peers.

Even if you reach the pinnacle of your model of existence, you still need to belong. You need a peer group.

Learning to get what you want from people is preying on that need of every person to belong, as well as preying on the need to be special.

And so, even though we may not want to admit it, in the short span of recorded history, humans have changed little. The world around us gives us new inputs that we must deal with, but we still go around satisfying our needs in our same old tried and tested human ways.

How humans interact and what people do naturally to create comfort in times of stress have remained fundamentally consistent through the ages. That's why it is possible to codify the means whereby you can get someone to do what you want in an amazing spectrum of circumstances. In this book, I insisted that you can only master the ability to get someone to do what you want if you understand the operation of the two primary social drives in human beings: the need to belong, and the need to differentiate one's self from the crowd.

Your success relative to others involves moving them up and down the tiers of these two needs by using the methods and strategies of interrogators. By applying the skills in the book, you can achieve an even greater success: you can help yourself understand your own needs and wants.

Everything we talked about applies to you as well as your targets. If you need to belong, use the tools to find common ground with people around you, and help them to understand who you are. If you need to differentiate, you can choose to participate in groups where you have extraordinary expertise.

The greatest lesson in this book may be applying the section on paring options to your own life and understanding when you are using the Landrum Factor on yourself. Remove that limiting practice, and you greatly expand your options for fulfilling your Maslow needs.

Manipulating people to do what you want takes cooperation, and there is always the element of unpredictability, because you naturally project parts of yourself onto someone else. We all do it. So, the best application of this book may be to yourself.

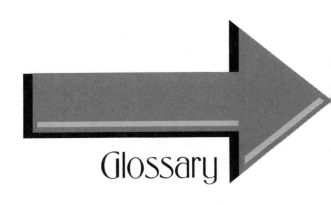

Glossary

Adaptors—Gestures to release stress and to adjust the body as a way to increase the comfort level.

Barriers—Postures and gestures we use when we are uncomfortable.

Baselining—Determining how a person behaves and speaks under normal circumstances.

Bell curve—A graphic representation of normal distribution, used in this book as a simple model for analyzing a group.

Belonging/love—Needs in the middle of Maslow's Hierarchy. (*See also* Hierarchy of Needs.)

Bonding—A way to exploit the two big needs of belonging and differentiating. (*See also* Fracturing.)

Compound question—A question that asks two or more questions at once.

Control question—A question to which you know the answer.

Differentiation/esteem—Needs just above belonging in Maslow's Hierarchy. (*See also* Hierarchy of Needs.)

Fracturing—A way to exploit the two big needs of belonging and differentiating. (*See also* Bonding)

Hierarchy of Needs (a.k.a. Maslow's Hierarchy)—Developed by Abraham Maslow to describe five levels of needs, from the most basic physiological needs to the highest human need of self-actualization; his theory is that one cannot move up to a higher level until the needs of the lower levels are met.

Illustrators—Gestures used to punctuate a statement.

Landrum Factor—Way of describing operational principles of paring options that was created for this book; the effect of the Landrum Factor is depicted in a narrow band of options running through the center of the overlapped Hierarchy of Needs and matrix of fulfillment.

Leading question—A question that projects the answer in the question.

Matrix of fulfillment—Visual system of depicting the phenomenon that the more options that exist, the higher someone progresses on the Hierarchy of Needs; conversely, fewer exist the lower a person is on the Hierarchy.

Mechanics of charisma—System of creating charisma introduced in this book

Personal extinction—The point at which self-image has been decimated.

Prototypical—A class of person that seems far above normal humanity; Greek gods are classic representations.

Regulators—Gestures used to control another person's speech.

Repeat question—The same question asked in different words.

Self-actualization—Need at the top of Maslow's Hierarchy. (*See also* Hierarchy of Needs.)

Source lead—Information dropped by someone in the course of conversation that the questioner feels there is value in pursuing.

Sub-typical—A person or group of people who fall on the left side of the bell curve in mapping a group.

Super-typical—A person or group of people who fall on the right side of the bell curve in mapping a group.

3-D bell curve—System of human modeling created for this book; overlaying multiple bell curves in a 3-D way; a kind of topographical map of who a person is.

Vague question—A fuzzy question that could simply be a badly phrased question, one used to distract from a topic, or one the questioner uses to bait a person into talking.

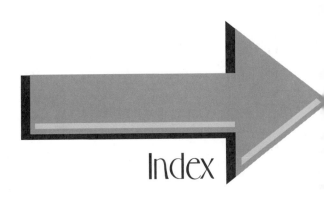

Index

About the Authors

Gregory Hartley's expertise as an interrogator first earned him honors with the U.S. Army. More recently, it has drawn organizations such as the CIA and national TV to seek his insights about "how to" as well as "why."

Hartley has an illustrious military record, including earning the prestigious Knowlton Award, which recognizes individuals who have contributed significantly to the promotion of Army Intelligence. He graduated from the U.S. Army Interrogation School, the Anti-Terrorism Instructor Qualification Course, the Principle Protection Instructor Qualification Course, several Behavioral Symptom Analysis Seminars, and SERE (Survival, Evasion, Resistance, Escape) school. His skills as an expert interrogator earned praise while he served as SERE Instructor, Operational Interrogation Support to the

5th Special Forces Group during operation Desert Storm, Interrogation Trainer, and as a creator and director of several joint-force, multinational interrogation exercises from 1994 to 2000. Among his military awards are the Meritorious Service Medal (which he received twice), Army Commendation Medal (of which he is a five-time recipient), Army Achievement Medal (which he received four times), National Defense Service Medal, Southwest Asia Service Medal, and Kuwait Liberation Medal. He also attended law school at Rutgers University.

Hartley has provided expert interrogation analysis for major network and cable television, particularly Fox News, as well as National Public Radio and prime print media such as *The Washington Post* and *Philadelphia Inquirer*. Important foreign media such as *Der Spiegel* have also relied on his commentary.

— — — — — —

Maryann Karinch is the author of 12 books, including five co-authored with Greg Hartley, namely *How to Spot a Liar* (Career Press, 2005), *I Can Read You Like a Book* (Career Press, 2007), *The Date Decoder* (Adams Media, 2008), *How to Be an Expert on Anything in Two Hours* (AMACOM, 2008), and *Get People to Do What You Want*.

Others published works are *Dr. David Sherer's Hospital Survival Guide* (with co-author David Sherer, MD; Claren Books, 2003); *Diets Designed for Athletes* (Human Kinetics, 2001); *Empowering Underachievers: How to Guide Failing Kids (8–18) to Personal Excellence* (co-author Dr. Peter Spevak;

New Horizon Press, 2000); *Lessons from the Edge: Extreme Athletes Show You How to Take on High Risk and Succeed* (Simon & Schuster, 2000); *Boot Camp: The Sergeant's Fitness and Nutrition Program* (with co-author Patrick "The Sarge" Avon; Simon & Schuster, 1999); and *Telemedicine: What the Future Holds When You're Ill* (New Horizon Press, 1994).

Earlier in her career, she managed a professional theater and raised funds for arts and education programs in Washington, D.C. She holds bachelor's and master's degrees in speech and drama from The Catholic University of America in Washington, D.C.

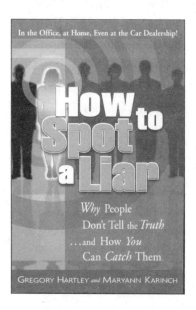

GREGORY HARTLEY AND MARYANN KARINCH

I Can Read You Like a Book

How to Spot the Messages and Emotions People Are Sending With Their Body Language

EAN 978-1-56414-941-1
US $15.99 (Can. $19.95)

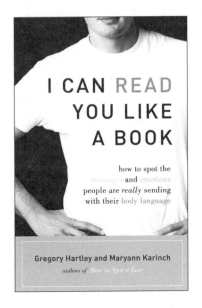

I CAN READ YOU LIKE A BOOK

how to spot the messages and emotions people are *really* sending with their body language

Gregory Hartley and Maryann Karinch
authors of How to Spot a Liar

"The best spies have street smarts and an intuitive understanding of the human psyche. This revealing book shows how anybody can put these skills to use in everyday life."

—Thomas Boghardt, historian,
International Spy Museum,
Washington, D.C.